Answers
for Elk Hunters

Jay Houston

Author of these leading books on elk hunting:

Elk Hunting 101, A Pocketbook Guide to Elk Hunting

Elk Hunting 201, Big Bulls…Essentials For A Successful Hunt

Elk Hunting 301, Making It Happen…In Elk Country

Ultimate Elk Hunting, Strategies, Techniques & Methods

A Hunter's Field Notes (with Roger Medley)

Elk Hunter, The Silver Bullet

Answers for Elk Hunters

Jay Houston

Copyright 2009-2016 by
Jay Houston / Author
Revised 2016

Our front cover photo is courtesy of Jerry Gowins.

Printed in the United States of America

ISBN 978-0-9759319-5-0
Jackson Creek Media Group, Inc.

Introduction

My focus in this book is to respond to <u>your</u> <u>questions</u> on elk hunting. *Answers for Elk Hunters* provides you with the real "meat and potatoes" information that hunters like you want to know.

Over the years, I have formed relationships with some of the most successful elk hunters and industry professionals on the planet. As required, I reach out to these hunters and professionals to get their thoughts and opinions in order to provide those who have asked the questions within with a well-rounded viewpoint. No one has all of the right answers, and I am no exception. If your opinion or that of someone else differs from those found in this book, great. Then I strongly encourage you to gather all of the information that you can, from as many reliable sources as you have at your disposal, and make your own best informed decision.

In *Answers for Elk Hunters*, I have also partnered with the hunting public. You have provided me with the great questions on elk hunting that are found within the pages of this book. For the public's generous contribution to this effort, I am exceedingly grateful. Thank you for allowing me the opportunity to respond with answers that I believe will help you to become a more successful elk hunter.

Safe Hunting & God Bless,

Jay

Why is there no Table of Contents?

The format I have chosen to use in *Answers for Elk Hunters* may seem a bit unconventional. You will not find a table of contents in this book, nor will you find information segmented into conventional chapters.

Rather those golden nuggets of information that are contained within are sprinkled randomly just as the questions were originally submitted to me. I have made great efforts to endeavor to leave the questions that were submitted just as I received them. In a few cases I used a limited amount of editorial license to make the question easier to read or understand. Whenever one of my contributors inadvertently gave away a bit more information about where he was hunting than he planned to, I provided a small amount of editorial snipping there as well.

Don't miss a ton of great recipes for elk at the back of the book!

Acknowledgements

First and foremost I want to praise God for having blessed me with this wonderful life that I am so privileged to live and share with my wife Rae Ann, my family, and so many others.

I want to thank my loving and beautiful wife Rae Ann without whose faithful encouragement would this work or any of our previous books ever have seen the light of day. You are the best!

Finally, I want to honor and pay tribute to my dad, Jim Houston, who nurtured the passion that God instilled in me for hunting and the high country. Love you Dad.

Answers for Elk Hunters

Q. **"Our group of hunters is scheduled to hunt the second rifle season in Colorado and camp at 11,000 feet within an elk migration route. When does migration typically occur and how much weather does it take to make the elk move?"**

Jeff, Oklahoma

A. Generally speaking Jeff, the elk migration is believed to be triggered by a combination of weather and the presence of significant amounts of snow in the higher elevations that hinders the elk in their search for food sources. Elk are opportunistic in their feeding habits. That means that they will seek out the best sources of food for the least amount of effort. Thus, if they have to dig down through a lot of snow to get at the forage beneath, they begin looking for food that is easier to get to. Generally speaking snow levels farther down the mountain are not as deep as those found higher up in the elk's summer range. A fairly good rule of thumb is when the snow gets as high as an elk's belly and stays at that depth, then the elk begin moving towards areas where the food sources are easier to get to, i.e. the migration. If the elk herd in your area is migratory, and not all are, then the locals will be able to give you a better feel for when the migration has occurred in the past. Second rifle season in Colorado is probably a bit early to expect elk to migrate but again that depends upon the specific area and the weather. In most cases, I would expect the elk to still be in their summer range during mid to late October.

Q. "I am going to hunt Colorado during the first rifle season this year and it will be my first elk hunt ever. What one thing could you advise me that would be the most beneficial to increase the possibility of my getting a shot at a bull."

Mike, Ohio

A. As a first time elk hunter you may want to keep these three things in mind: First, pay very close attention to the wind all the time. Wind direction can and will change on you very quickly in the high country changing your position of advantage to one of disadvantage. There are few things that will adversely affect your hunt faster than a bad wind. Second, you will need to pace yourself. The air is a lot thinner above 7,000 feet and it will wear you out quickly if you do not take your time, hydrate, and eat well. Keep in mind that eating a lot and eating well is not the same thing. Effective elk hunting requires your body to burn huge amounts of energy every day, so you will need to replenish that burned fuel with more high energy fuel. Carbohydrates are an excellent source of such fuel. Finally, be aggressive. Do not wait for the elk to come to you like you sometimes see on TV, take the initiative and move in as close as you can get...then get closer still.

Q. "This past weekend (Archery Season) I packed in to elk camp. The first evening I decided to try some calling and got a bull to answer. I called him across a drainage and the bull closed to within 200 yards. He would only answer to a bugle and not a cow call. After numerous attempts to call the bull in closer, darkness ended any chance we might have had for a successful encounter. I assume the rut was not on since he wasn't answering to the cow call, or I didn't close the distance to get a shot?"

Josh, Idaho

A. Bulls do not always answer cow calls for a host of reasons especially if the rut hasn't kicked in yet. When a bull hangs up like this, it is usually best to stop calling and make a plan for closing the distance yourself. Far too many hunters are hesitant to become aggressive in such a situation. Next time he hangs up, check the wind, determine a route that will get you within range and go after him. If you can get within 100 yards or so and hit him with a spike squeal, sometimes this will trigger an aggressive response and the bull will move towards you thinking that some young bull has slipped in on him. Herd bulls can get pretty worked up over something like this. This tactic is usually only good one time. If this doesn't work, I would try very quiet cow calling directed to one side or another of your setup. The idea here is to get the bull to come towards you but to one side or the other. Make sure you try to get him to pass you upwind! Then be quiet and hope he comes in. If not, you have two choices, back out quietly and try again tomorrow or go just for it.

Q. "Do elk tend to bed up in cover during rainy weather or does it not effect on their movement...and if so where does one need to look for them in rainy weather?"

Mark, Tennessee

A. How the elk will behave in this type of situation can really depend upon the amount of rain. While a light drizzle may have little effect on elk movement, a good heavy rain or a thunderstorm is likely to push the elk back into cover. If hail is involved, as is often the case in the high country, the sound of the hail coming through the over story reduces an elk's ability to hear danger and the elk get pretty edgy. They can hardly wait to get back out of the cover in such a case. Storms can be a tremendous asset to the elk hunter who is willing to wait it out without returning to camp. If there are elk in the area, it has been my experience that they almost always break cover soon after a big storm. In addition, storms are usually accompanied by significant changes in barometric pressure (a drop) and gusty surface winds. These weather phenomena can precede a storm by as much as 150 miles. The elk will notice both, causing an increase in the amount of movement as they feed in preparation for the storm. Rather than try to sneak up on elk in heavy cover during a storm, I would suggest watching the fringes of cover after the storm.

Q. "Our rifle season starts here in October. The area that we plan to hunt has limited campsites. Therefore we will be forced to camp close to the area that we plan to hunt. What is your recommendation regarding a camp fire? We expect that the weather by then will be in the 20-30s at night. Although we have a wall tent and LOTS of needed sleeping equipment, a fire would be nice for added warmth in the evenings."

Jo Ella, Colorado

A. I love a camp fire. The camaraderie experienced and stories told around a nice fire have been an essential ingredient in elk camps for centuries. That being said, your decision on whether to build a fire or not really depends upon how close you really are to the area you plan to hunt. Camp fires do not smell like wildfires. Their smell predisposes the elk to your presence in their territory. If you are measuring close in yards (less than a mile), then I would suggest you to do without the fire. If you are measuring in miles, then go for it. Be sure that you are aware of any fire restrictions that may be in place at the time. Also don't hang out around the fire in your hunting duds, as they tend to absorb the smell of the fire.

Q. "Just skimmed your Elk Hunting 101 book - great stuff! I was fortunate enough to be invited elk hunting late last year, and I must not have been too annoying, because I was invited again, for the first two weekends in muzzle loading season. Other than "be quiet and don't move"

any advice for the girlfriend going along on the elk hunt? I won't be behind the gun, but I will have binoculars and range finder. Thanks!"

Michelle, Colorado

A. I am impressed! I would offer two thoughts; first, since you are new to this, make sure that you and your clothing are as scent free as possible for the entire time you are in elk camp. Gals have a whole different set of priorities when it comes to the way they smell. The biggest gotcha for "gals" is usually their hair; if you can avoid the use of any scented products like shampoo, mousse, etc. that would be very good. The other thought is that you become a valuable asset to whoever you are hunting with because your presence adds a second set of eyes to the equation. Rather than focusing on your significant other when you are in the woods, try sitting facing the other way while you look for elk. This way you become a valued part of the hunting team rather than someone your hunting partner has to watch out for. Way to go, Michelle.

Q. "I will be elk hunting this year for the first time and thought a good elk scent would help. I am not sure of too many people that make elk scents. Suggestions?"

Anonymous

A. There are literally hundreds of products on the market that claim to be good for attracting bulls or covering your own scent. Many of us who live in elk country, however, have found two excellent cover scents that work well. The good news is that you can find them almost everywhere and they are free. Pine needle oil and sage are excellent natural cover scents. Both have an oil-like base that will stick to your clothing. All you have to do is grab a handful of either and rub it on your gear. For a longer lasting effect, take some along with you by sticking it in your daypack.

Q. **"When you are stand hunting from the ground, do you need to conceal yourself, or will your camo be sufficient if you are sitting up against a tree? Or can we hunt from ground blinds in Colorado?"**

AJ, Colorado

A. Most of us lean toward as much concealment as possible while keeping a selection of shooting lanes available. Sometimes leaning up against a bush or tree is the best you can get. In this case try to have actual contact with the tree. This prevents the elk from seeing movement between the tree and you. Ground blinds usually only work when you have located a well used resource like a wallow or watering hole. If there are indicators that elk are using this area daily, then construct a ground setup making sure to take prevailing wind into account. Study how the elk are getting into and out of the area as well before placing your stand. Don't rely solely on the camo pattern of a commercial ground blind. Locate natural material such as branches, leaves or grass and place these on and around the blind.

Q. **"Two times this past month I have missed opportunities while archery hunting for cow elk. Herds of elk have been found in the morning with all sorts of bugling and mewing going on. The wind was not good for a stalk both times. We waited until evening. In the PM the** wind was great and we were able to get in close to where the elk had been in the morning but there was no sign of the herd (40 or so) at all. This was mid week and there was no reason for them to get blown out. No other hunters in area, no sign of predators. We hiked back out both times and did small location bugles in surrounding canyons within six miles in the dark. Not a mew, bugle or a bark anywhere. Where did they go? Any thoughts on what we could do better? We did not over call, in fact we didn't even call in one circumstance. The bulls were very active. There was no change in the weather at all. This herd has always stayed within a mile of the ridges and bowls we see them in."

Mike, Utah.

A. It's possible that you were catching the elk early as they were preparing to enter their bedding area. It may be that by the time you got to where the herd was in the morning, they had already moved away from that area and back towards their evening feeding area. While elk are primarily nocturnal feeders, during the fall the amount of time they actually feed at night increases by about 20 percent. This means that they starting heading to those feeding areas earlier. I would make a plan to be in place where you saw them in the very early morning pre-dawn hours. This will probably require that you leave camp far earlier than you have in the past. I have had to leave camp as early as 2:00 a.m. in some cases, so that I would be in place before the elk showed up in the early morning.

Q. "If you glass a mountain late in the evening and spot elk, what should you do at that point? Be in that spot early

the next morning? Continue to glass the next morning in that same location to determine their movements such as are they moving from bedding area to feeding area in hope of setting up and ambush? Had this situation a week ago and was not sure what to do."

Dave, Missouri

A.I suggests that you consider constructing a plan to be setup the following evening near where you spotted the elk. If you have the time, I would return to the same vantage point where you initially spotted them the following morning to see if they are still where you saw them the evening before. From there you may be able to determine their movement pattern. This could give you a lot more information for planning that evening stalk.

Q. "I am archery hunting in southwestern Colorado and I have noticed I can't raise a bugle from a bull and haven't heard any bugling even at night. I have asked around and it seems I am not the only one having this problem. What should I do? Have the elk become immune to the call?"

Shawn, Colorado

A. There could be any number of reasons for the bulls being quiet. 1) They just haven't decided to start talking yet...they will sooner or later, but if their testosterone level is not high enough yet, all the cow calling in the world won't change it. 2) I don't know what your calling sounds like, but that could be an issue. 3) If there are a lot of predators in the area, elk will stay quiet for obvious reasons. You are probably going to have to wait them out. In that you are so far south, they may not start talking for another couple of weeks because the runt tents to start later the further south you are.

Q. "I have been archery hunting elk for 14 years as an Idaho resident. Because time and money are in short supply for me I am forced to hunt close to home. A good portion of my hunting is done around a little town in north Idaho, which has been, in the last couple of years become home to many wolves. I have been having a hard time locating elk the past few years with calls they seem to be talking less and herding in smaller herds during the rut. I was wondering if this has anything to do with the wolves. I am also interested in any tips for hunting in wolf country when the elk are not callable. Any suggestions are greatly appreciated."

Tim, Idaho

A. If there is any significant number of wolves (a pack) in the area, the elk will in all likelihood be elsewhere. If that is the case, you will need to find another place to hunt. Additionally, you can rest assured that any elk remaining in the area will likely remain quiet.

Q. "What are the best calls/brands to carry afield? I'm going to Wyoming in a few weeks and want to hear from the experts...their opinion."

Vinny, New York

A. There are a whole lot of great elk calls on the market. I've used most. Diaphragm mouth calls are the best type of call but they are also the toughest to learn to use well. Wayne Carlton,

Bugling Bull, Knight and Hale, and Primos make excellent calls, to name a few. Since you are heading out in a few weeks I would suggest you beat feet to your nearest sporting goods store ASAP as you are way behind the power curve if you are planning on using a call and have yet to purchase one or practice with it. Try a couple of reed type calls. There are open reed and closed reed calls, each will produce a different type of cow call. Again, Knight and Hale, Carlton, Hunters Specialties, and Primos all make great calls. One of my favorites however is a Sceery Ace-1 cow call (the camo one). Also the Primos Hoochi Mama is always a good simple to use call to fall back on. Buy a call with a CD and practice from now until you arrive in camp. Pay close attention to the instructions on the CD about when to call and when to be quiet. Most CDs have some 'real elk" talk on them. I like to listen to the elk talking and try to mimic them.

Q. "What's the best strategy for hunting elk during a full moon phase? I'm hunting the Colorado muzzleloading season where we will have a full moon."

Jim, Indiana

A. I know that there are a lot of folks that will disagree with me on this, but in my nearly 25 years of elk hunting I have not found moon phase to have any significant affect on elk behavior. This is not the case with whitetail as I am sure you know. Elk are primarily nocturnal feeders 365 days a year. It doesn't matter whether the moon is full, quarter, or waning, they still feed mostly at night. During the hunting season, they increase the amount of time they spend feeding during nighttime hours by about 20%, but that is about it. Some folks like to attribute moon phases to everything they hunt, however the idea that moon phases play a significant role in elk feeding habits isn't supported by the consensus of experience. I have a very good friend who is one of the best elk outfitters in CO who will disagree with me on this. He is a great friend and outfitter and we just agree to disagree.

Q. "We are going for elk during 4th rifle in Colorado. Are water bladders practical or will they freeze up?"

Keith, Tennessee

A. Never leave camp without your hydration bladder. Bladders have a number of advantages over canteens or water bottles. First they usually hold a lot more water. Second, as they empty they collapse and keep the water from sloshing around as you walk. Finally, having the mouthpiece close at hand allows you to hydrate more often and with far less movement, that might give away your position. Keeping yourself hydrated is critical when hunting at higher elevations. Unlike deer hunting from a treestand, elk hunting requires endless hours of traversing all types of terrain, very little of which is level ground. The bladder will not freeze as you hunt during the day, and usually only freezes at night if left outside the tent. If it does freeze, not to worry, it will thaw out in short order from the body heat as you hike up the mountain. **TIP**: If your hydration bladder is not empty at the end of the day when you get back to camp, then you are not drinking enough. Trust me on this!

Q. "Jay, what do you think about using scent management clothing products for elk?"

Anonymous

If you have a fresh set they can work to your advantage for a while. Here is the problem. Most of this type of gear was originally designed for whitetail deer hunting where hunters can drive to within a short walk of a favorite treestand or ground blind and setup for the day. Such a hike is not usually that physically demanding and rarely works up a good sweat. On the other hand, if your gear is saturated with odor, as will be the case after a few days of hard hunting and walking 6-10 miles up and down mountains in the high country, then it will not provide you with the same level of protection that it did when it was fresh. A sponge will only absorb so much. If you have two sets I would bring them both along. Remember, just because you are wearing scent management clothing or using some sort of cover scent, don't let your guard down and forget that you must always know where the wind is and use it to your advantage. There is no substitute for hunting smart.

Q. "My group and I hunt south Eastern Washington just north of the Oregon border. We hike miles into the forest usually between the end of October and the beginning of November at an elevation of around 5,500 feet. I use my cow call to try and stir up some elk. Is this a good thing to do? Does it help to cow call during this time of year or am I just tooting my own horn to make noise and scaring away any potential elk?"

Todd, Washington

A. Cow elk are vocal 365 days a year. When you use your cow call, you are just trying to start a conversation. The idea here is to get a cow to talk back and let you know where she is. Then you plan a stalk. Effective elk talk is more about knowing when to call and when not too. A major mistake is that of overcalling. This ain't duck huntin'. Try throwing out a few cow calls, wait a minute, and repeat. If nothing, move on a few hundred yards and try again. If you repeat this cycle three times and get no response, I would give it a rest and try the same sequence after an hour or so or perhaps in a different drainage. The TV shows make elk calling appear to be much easier than it actually is. What you do not see on TV or a DVD is the many, many hours of hunting and calling with nothing happening before the action starts. This part of the tape never makes it out of editing. All of this assumes that the hunter actually knows how to use an elk call. That is not something that we can teach here. If you have a question about this, consider buying one of the many excellent calling CDs on the market. Sceery, Primos, Bugling Bull, Hunters Specialties, Knight and Hale all make great training CDs, just to name a few.

Q. "This year elk season started a week later than last year. My question is when are elk in the peak of the rut? Does it change every year?"

Dave, Missouri

A. There is no calendar date that defines the "peak of the rut." Since you are bowhunting and already out there it really isn't going to make much difference. Bull elk enter the rut based up a certain level of testosterone in their brain which is triggered by photoperiod or the day/night (light/dark) cycle. If I want to hunt the peak of the rut in northern Colorado, I usually plan on the last 10 days in September. If you are hunting farther north, the rut may come a bit earlier, if farther south a bit later.

Q. "If I am hunting in 70-80 degree weather in September how long do I have to get the elk to the butcher after I skin and quarter it?"

Mike, Washington

A. Your best bet is to get it to a cooler as soon as possible. In many cases however, that just is not practical as you are on the mountain for a week or more. Bacteria begins building in the carcass the minute the heart stops, so get the critter opened up, skinned, and quartered ASAP. This helps to begin cooling the meat. If there is snow, use this to help in the cooling down process by packing the meat with snow. When you get the meat back to camp, hoist the meat bags up in a tree in the dark shade to keep predators off. Regardless of daytime temps, nighttime temps in the high country usually dip low enough to keep your meat cool until you are ready to haul it back down the mountain. We have stored meat like this for as long as 5 days with no spoilage at all. Make sure to use heavy duty game bags, one for each quarter.

Q. "My question is in Oregon & Washington our cougar population has more than tripled its size in the last several years. I am a little nervous of this. What are the odds of being attacked by a cougar while venturing deep in the timber? Is it more likely they would prefer praying on game than humans?"

JJB, Washington

A. I have hiked and hunted in mountain lion country for almost 25 years and never had an encounter with a cat. While I know that they may be around, we have managed to avoid one another. Humans are not in the food chain of a healthy cat. Older cats and injured cats that can no longer hunt deer and other game that are a normal part of their food chain, and real young cats that are just stupid are the ones we read about. Unfortunately, we do not have access to stats on individual states. You might check with the Game and Fish folks. I don't give bears or cats a second thought when I am elk hunting. Note: I don't hunt in grizzly country...that is a whole different animal.

Q. "I want to shoot a bull elk. Size is not an issue. What season would be the best if the hunter is accomplished in Archery, Muzzleloader or Rifle? What if I wanted to just meat hunt and shoot a cow?"

Cole, Colorado

A. What season is best? This depends to a large extent which weapon you prefer to hunt with. All seasons offer excellent opportunities. That being said, archery and muzzleloading seasons are usually earlier and offer the hunter the opportunity to hunt the rut. Bulls are far more vocal during this time, thus they are easier to locate. Since they are somewhat distracted by their desire to procreate, a smart stealthy hunter may stand a better chance of sneaking in for a shot. If I wanted to just meat hunt for a cow, I would pick a late season during the migration in the area you plan to hunt. This is usually later in November or even December. At this time, most hunters have gone home, the elk are no longer focused on the rut, and they are moving from their summer range to winter range usually in large visible numbers.

Q. "How much pressure does it take an elk before they leave an area with great food, water, and shelter? Will they travel out totally before winter if people are going through their territory?"

JD, Colorado

A. Elk don't usually leave their summer range totally until the weather makes it too difficult to locate and access good forage. Hunting pressure will definitely affect their travel patterns however. Usually what the elk will move into areas that are less accessible to hunters, i.e. heavy dark timber, deep holes, or a drainage that has less hunting pressure. It's important to keep in mind that the "great food, water, and shelter" that you speak of is at the top of their list of priorities. If you are hunting an area that gets a lot of hunting pressure, consider hunting from a spike camp and packing in to get away from the majority of the other hunters. If this is not practical for you, you may have to consider hunting some of those less friendly pieces of ground that I mentioned earlier.

Q. "How can you tell a young antlerless bull from a cow?"

TM, Wisconsin

A. By the taste! There is no better eating than a young bull. As a rule, male elk (yearlings) do not begin to develop antlers until May-June in the year following their birth. Therefore male calves will be without antlers during the fall of their first year. A good clue should be the actual size of the animal. If it's a full body sized elk in the fall and without antlers, then your chances are very good that it is a cow.

Q. "What is the preferred food for elk in the middle of the Colorado Rocky Mountains?"

Tom, Colorado

A. If I were to tell you: Common commandra, or Velvet lupine or Yellowhair crazyweed, it probably wouldn't help much. I've tried this on hunters in the fields, and in 100% of the cases no one knew the names of any plant that elk like to eat. Plus the plant type that may be in abundance in one part of Colorado may not be available at all in another area. Fall (hunting season) is the time that elk use to store up as much fat (energy) as possible in order to survive the coming winter months when forage is much harder to find. While elk are primarily grazers they can switch to browse if necessary to find the high quality forage they need. Practically speaking look for new growth grasses which are high in nutrient content. By new growth I mean grass that has only recently come up, say ten inches or less. Look for these near seeps and springs, on the floor of timbered areas, and along the edges of timber. There is a lot more on this in my book, *Elk Hunting 301*.

Q. "When trying to locate elk in a new area by calling using cow calls, herd talk and location bugling... what is the sequence and duration of each type of call that you suggest using before moving to the next calling location?"

Mike, Pennsylvania.

A. The answer is sort of like what is the best line to use when trying to strike up a conversation with someone new...whatever works! Expect some trial and error in the process. Try a ten second sequences of gentle cow calls...mews. Use more than one call to simulate a number of different cows conversing, nothing aggressive at first. Space these out over time and location. Remember the purpose is to 'locate' the elk. In most cases I reserve bugling for locator calls. A sequence of two or three bugles may get the interest of a bull that will respond and bugle back letting you know where he is. That's about 70% of the job. Don't wait and try to draw him in, make the move in his direction yourself. Always monitor the wind and keep it in your favor. This is critical. Close the distance, and then start the cow calling again. If he starts to come in, it helps to have a decoy (Montana if you have it) so that the bull can actually see who he is talking to. If he gets close and fails to see anything, he may hang up. If you don't have a store bought decoy, use a light brown burlap feed bag draped over a bush upwind of your setup. Patience, persistence, and endurance are the name of the game.

Q. "I usually hunt early September in order to have a better opportunity to get into bulls before they cow up. The problem is I seem to have trouble finding them, help?"

Anonymous

A. During the dog days of early September, the high daytime temps will usually keep the elk will hold up in the dark timber to avoid the heat and the flies. They typically begin heading back to these bedding areas before sunrise. If you don't want to hunt them in the dark stuff, you have to find out where they are going into it and be in place as they come back up the mountain. Otherwise, you have to go into the dark timber for the elk. On those hot days elk can stay in the timber from before sun up until after sunset.

Q. "In planning our elk trip for the end of October here in Southeast Washington State, we were planning on going for a scouting weekend the second weekend of September. Is this a good idea or is waiting a little longer say the last weekend of September be a better idea? That would be a month prior to our rifle season."

Todd, Washington

A. A little research into when elk move from summer range to winter range in your area might be a good investment of your time. I haven't hunted elk in Washington State. In Colorado, New Mexico, Wyoming, Montana, Utah, and Idaho, elk will start to migrate from their summer range to winter range when the snow makes getting to forage more trouble than the elk want to put up with. If the weather (snow) hasn't started the migration then the elk will probably be using some of the same drainages in September that they use in October. If that is the case your planned scouting trip would work fine.

Q. "How do I tell the differences between bull and cow elk droppings when I'm hunting or scouting? How fresh do droppings need to be to indicate that elk are in an area?"

Anonymous

A. The taste...just kidding. Usually cow droppings are tapered on both ends, whereas bull droppings usually have a dimpled-in look to one end. Also, and this is a general rule, if you are seeing droppings scattered rather than clumped, that can be an indicator of elk under stress. Fresh droppings are usually soft and green if the elk are grazing. If they have switched to browse, they may be soft and brown. If the droppings are black, the elk are very likely gone.

Q. "Do bull elk bugle as a challenge to other bulls?"

Anonymous

A. Bugling is a form of male advertisement. When a bull elk bugles he is communicating to all the cow elk within hearing range that he is available and he is "the guy" that they are looking for. He is also verbally staking his claim to his harem and the territory. In the elk mating ritual, it is the cow that chooses with which bull she will mate, thus the bull is continually reinforcing his importance and dominance within the herd.

Q. "Last week I located a bull by calling. He was about 300 yards away give or take. Not sure what to do; set up my Montana elk decoy and make cow call sounds or move in slowly as close as possible then begin cow calling."

Dave, Missouri

A. I would lean more on option #2, move in slowly. You did not mention if the bull was alone, with other bulls, or has cows already. If the latter, it will be very difficult for you to pull him away from his herd, which makes more of an argument for you trying to sneak in. Keep in mind that if he has cows, your plan will have to take into account the cows as well as any raghorn bulls that may be lurking about. Never forget the wind! Once you get within 100 yards, setup the decoy upwind and try a couple of soft cow calls followed by a spike squeal. Sometimes this is just more than a lonely bull can take and he comes running.

Q. "We are going to be hunting private land in Colorado during the third rifle season. The land is above public land. The property has Aspen trees, pastures, a cypress hillside and a tank on it. Where should we hunt the hardest? Three years ago we killed a nice bull coming out of a pasture into the Aspens."

Brian, Texas

A. Look for the elk to hold up primarily on the dark timbered north and east facing slopes during the day. By the time third rifle season rolls around, the elk can be a little spooked so they will bed down early, possibly before shooting light and they may not come back out until just before dark. If the ranch that you are hunting is a pretty good size and holds a resident herd, this may not be the case if the elk have not been hunted heavily. If so, look for elk in areas with new growth forage (really green and ten inches or less in height). The elk are really trying to pack on the carbs at this time of the year, so food is what they are most interested in. The larger bulls may have gotten back together in bachelor groups. These boys will remain high on the mountain for as long as possible until deep snows drive them down.

Q. "One of my favorite hunting drainages in the heavily timbered Pacific Northwest got badly burned out last year. There is still a lot of standing live timber (good

cover), and there are certainly patches of grass that are coming back , but the game trails have vanished--a few sporadic prints here and there, but no more heavy activity. Question: how many years will it take until the Elk move back in? Given feed and cover and water, why are they still gone now?"

Kevin, Idaho

A. As a rule, burns are usually excellent places to hunt for about three years starting about three months after the fire. This is due to all the new growth that is usually abundant. Elk love it. The absence of elk could be due to any number of reasons: Hunting pressure, active logging in the area, an increase of predators in the area, especially if a wolf pack considers the burn a part of their home range. Something to keep in mind when hunting burns: Cow elk prefer larger burned out areas so that they can move out into the middle keeping a fair amount of distance away from the tree line. Elk still have a plains game defense mentality, so the cows want to be able to see danger coming a long way off. Bulls, on the other hand, have a different defense mechanism, i.e., their antlers. They don't mind a fight if it comes down to it, so bulls can sometimes be found in smaller burns.

Q. "Unfortunately I will only be able to hunt the first two days of the first rifle season here in Colorado. Would my best bet at a cow be to run and gun or sit tight and let other hunters try and push elk my way?"

Bryan, Colorado

A. Unless there is a compelling reason to sit on a spot for two days such as an actively used wallow or waterhole, I would run and gun. This allows you to cover far more territory thus potentially exposing yourself to a lot more elk. If you sit tight, the only elk you are going to encounter are those that run in front of you...if any run in front of you.

Q. "I was on Gore Pass in Colorado all the last week of muzzleloader (2008). Saw a couple of young bucks and half a dozen does BUT not one elk was seen or heard by anyone the entire week. Moon was like a spotlight all week and people were talking of bad winter kill there last winter. It rained off and on so no draught, lots of water. We hunted around 9,500 feet. We even resorted to getting out at night and looking around and driving and saw zero. Beef cows in the area, too. What do you think? The temperature was 60s during the day and 35-40 at night."

Jim, Colorado

A. Here are a couple of thoughts. First if there are significant numbers of cattle in the area, the elk will not stay there. Cattle are way too much competition for the scarce forage that the elk are desperately trying to acquire at this time of the year. (See my book Elk Hunting 301 on this.) A few head rarely has any serious impact on elk numbers in a specific area, but a herd will pretty much end the hunting until they are pulled off of the mountain. In many areas in Colorado, ranchers will not finish roundup until early October, so bowhunters on public land have to deal with cattle. Second, the winter kill in that area was probably not significant enough to cause the lack of elk you describe. Third, and some have disagreed with me on this, the moon phase doesn't really make much difference to elk at all as they are nocturnal feeders 365 days a year. Fourth, the fact that you failed to hear elk is probably indicative of the rut not having really kicked in yet. My experience in hunting central Colorado is that the bulls do not begin to get vocal until the later part of September. The exception to this being park elk in Rocky Mountain National Park and they bugle all year long. Finally, depending upon the severity of the rain, this can keep the elk hold up in dark timber more than normal. Light rains don't usually make any difference, however during heavy rain and storms, the elk will hunker down. The daytime temps you indicated can also keep the elk hold up in the dark timber from before sunup to near dark as well.

Q. "I am a 55 year old man. I have been hunting elk since the 70's. I have been on guided and non-guided hunts throughout five states and as of yet I have not been successful. I have been very successful on mule deer hunts. I am planning to hunt Colorado in the 2008 season which I have hunted several times before. Do you have any suggestions?"

Doug, Iowa

A. There are two things I share with everyone who asked what do they need to do to become a more successful elk hunter. First, get in the best physical shape that you can so that you have the ability to hunt long and hunt hard. Second is to learn as much as possible about the elk themselves. These are basics. This is a lot more to learn, but without the basics, the rest is not going to make much of a difference in the outcome of your hunt. Make a pledge to yourself that you will go as far as it takes to get into the elk. Anything less will leave you with an empty freezer.

Q. "I am a first time elk and mule deer hunter and I am going to Colorado for the first time this year. What would be your suggestion on where to go and what public land to hunt on? I am going the first week of November. I just don't want to go blind. I would really appreciate it if you could help."

A. I am going to leave the name and state off of my response to this question for reasons that will become obvious. In over twelve years of trying to help folks become more successful elk hunters, this is fairly indicative of one of the questions I get asked the most. I am sure that the individual who asked this question did so with a very genuine desire to learn. The question however reflects almost no understanding of elk hunting or western hunting. The big game hunting populations in the USA is, give or take, about 80% deer hunters. Of the 20% balance only a portion are actually elk hunters. What portion I don't know. Folks who are into statistics estimate that there may be as many at 400,000 elk hunters. I personally think this is an overly optimistic number.

My best answer to the above question is, stay home this year. Get smart on elk hunting, do a lot of homework on where you would like to hunt, and begin planning your future hunt one year in advance. The 'hunter' above really is going into this effort blind. Even telling him exactly where to hunt would in all likelihood result in him coming home empty handed. Heading to elk camp without having done an adequate amount of homework is the same as taking a final exam in college without ever having stepped foot in the class. Is there any chance that this hunter could come home with an elk? Sure as there is no accounting for just happening to be in the right place at the right time. Reality however is that this hunter's chances of success are probably less than two percent...and that is being optimistic. Why, because he isn't adequately prepared.

Q. "I will be first time elk hunting in Colorado during the first rifle. I scouted two weeks ago and located two active wallows. Since this unit offered no early archery or muzzleloader hunts, would it be a good bet to key on this area, or are elk likely to move frequently from one area to another?"

Craig, Wisconsin

A. I would focus on the wallows as long as there is evidence that they are still in use. Active wallows stay trashed up, i.e. cloudy water, lots of tracks, torn up brush in the general area. If there is water in the wallow and it is clear, then it is probably not being used. Make sure that you maintain very tight control over your scent if you setup on a wallow. This may require that you move from time to time. You could set up a trailcam to see if elk are hitting the wallow. Two factors come into play that affect elk movement during hunting season, the need to find good forage and the need to avoid hunters. Both can and will cause elk to change their area and travel patterns.

Q. "Is calling after the rut helpful or should you be quiet and stalk?"

John, Virginia

A. After the rut, spot and stalk pretty much becomes the best way to locate elk. Bulls become much less vocal after the rut. A bull may have depleted up to 30% of his body fat during the course of the rut and he is tired. Rest and recuperation are the rule of the day for bulls during this time of the year. This usually means remaining quiet. I would stick with cow calling primarily as cows talk 365 days a year. If you get a response, get aggressive and move in always watching the wind. Your failure to manage the wind will end your hunt much faster than most other things.

Q. "I will be hunting elk second rifle season in Colorado. Do you recommend using calls to locate elk or since the rut is over will they respond? What type of calls would you recommend?"

Sean, Nebraska

A. Cow calling can work well year round for locating elk. If you know how to use a diaphragm call and can use it in conjunction with a grunt tube, this combo can work well for projecting your call across a fairly significant distance, which is usually the idea if you are "locating." Bugling after the rut rarely produces much in the way of positive results. It's important however, to keep in mind that in some years, depending where you are hunting, the rut can extend well into second or even third rifle season in Colorado. In this case it is a good idea to have a small bugle in your daypack.

I missed a rather long shot at a dandy 300 plus B&C bull on the second day of third rifle season in Colorado in 2006. It was early November and that bull still had three cows and a satellite bull with him and he was screaming his head off prior to my shot. His bugling was how we actually located him. I was fortunate enough however, to take a nice 5x6 bull the following day at 323 yards. This bull was lying on a bench and quietly watching us walk all the way across a draw right in front of him.

I carry a pretty good selection of calls with me including mouth diaphragms, open and closed reed calls, a Primos Pack Bugle, and usually a Primos Hoochie Mama™. I will try one call and if that one doesn't get their attention, I'll try another call and another until I've run through all the tricks in my bag. My favorite reed type call is the Sceery Ace 1™. Don't get me wrong, there are a lot of other great reed calls, but the Ace 1 was the first call I ever learned to use. Over many years of elk hunting, I have gone through three or four of these. They have become like an old friend and they do the job. Bugling Bull Game Calls and Knight and Hale make some excellent mouth diaphragms, and I really like my Primos Pack Bugle™. No matter how hard I blow the Pack Bugle, it will not intimidate younger bulls. It doesn't seem to have the horsepower to sound like the biggest bull in the valley and I prefer that.

Q. "I just got some new washable wool pants and shirt. My old stuff got moth eaten last winter. Work clothes I guess now. I like the look and feel of this new stuff, just hopes it holds up 25 years too. How do you keep moths out with no mothballs?"

Hank, California

A. Cedar is Mother Nature's repellant and has been a long-time favorite of many over the years for keeping moths off of wool and other garments when they are in storage. Cedar has a natural ability to repel not only insects but mildew as well. From time to time you will want to reactivate the aroma with a light sanding.

Q. "Ok, I'm asking the expert, and what he says, GOES. I will be elk/mule deer hunting in Colorado this year. This is my first trip out west so I need guidance on sighting in my rifle and grain of bullet. I will be using a 30-06. Everybody I talk to has an opinion, Sight at 200 yards, 2 inches high, sight dead on at 150, etc... Then there's the grain, 180+ or you're wasting your time, 165 grain at most. You get the point. So what do I do?"

Tim, Texas

A. Western hunting situations often present the hunter with shots far longer than most encountered while deer hunting in the Midwest or eastern United States. Shots of 250 plus yards are routine and shots of 350 plus yards are not all that rare. I would concur with your friend who suggested that you sight your rifle in to be dead on at 200 yards. Exactly how high you will be hitting at 100 yards will be determined by the exact round you are shooting. This ballistic information is readily available online on the website of your ammunition manufacturer. 165 grain and 180 grain bullets are both fine for elk. I prefer the 180 gr. Swift Scirocco™, but that is just my preference. More important than the weight of the round in grains is knowing how well that particular round will hold up on elk. Mass retention and good expansion are two critical elements in this equation. There are numerous excellent bonded bullets that meet this requirement. Also, available kinetic energy (KE) is very important. You want to make sure that you have a minimum of 1500 foot pounds of energy at impact. This too is available in the online ballistic tables. The point where the KE drops below the 1500 level becomes your maximum range. As you can see, a little research into the ballistics of your particular ammunition can give you quality insight.

Q. "I have a friend that recently (September) shot a very nice 7x6 bull with a bow. I know exactly where he shot it, but I won't be able to hunt until rifle season in mid-November. What are the chances that the herd will stay in the same area if they receive little pressure until then? It will be rifle deer season soon but no more elk until November. Do the herds move quite a lot naturally over this time? Also, do elk tend to move large distances during the day before they bed down every night?"

Anonymous, Oregon

A. Elk can and will move as much as necessary in search of quality food and security. How much they move in any area will depend upon each situation. When unpressured, elk may stay in a particular drainage for weeks at a time unless they exhaust the food sources. There is a pretty good chance that the elk will not be where your friend harvested his bull especially if there is any significant hunting pressure in that area. If you have access to a trailcam, you might put one up in the area near a water hole or wallow to see if the elk are still using it.

If your particular area experiences significant amounts of snowfall, i.e. twenty inches or more, the elk may begin to migrate from their summer grounds to their winter grounds. In this case they can cover significant distances, i.e. 20-50 miles or more.

Elk are primarily nocturnal feeders. During the fall when they have to really store up fat reserves, they may increase the amount of time that they feed at night by up to 20 percent. Elk may move miles from their nighttime feeding areas to their daytime bedding areas. A smart hunter will try to pattern the elk and locate a stand somewhere along that path.

Q. "We are hunting the 1st and 2nd rifle seasons in north central Colorado this year. It is the first time I have hunted in this area. We have done a lot of scouting, and found great sign and seen several elk. I have talked to bow hunters, muzzle loaders, and the game and parks, and found that there are elk in the area but there has been a lot of pressure and the elk are holding tight in the dark timber. I scouted the dark timber several times early and have hunted in dark timber before, but I have never been able to find where elk bed during the day. Do you have any suggestions on locating bedding areas in dark timber, because I have the feeling that is where I am going to have to head in order to find the bulls in my area?"

Justin, Colorado

A. The dark timber is exactly where the elk will head. Following the rut, three thoughts are on an elk's mind; high quality food, security, and rest and the dark timber provides all of these in most cases. Here is something to keep in mind. Throughout the day elk have need of water to aid in the digestive process. I would suggest looking for water sources, specifically sources that are contained within or flow through the dark timber such as streams, springs, or seeps. These sources not only provide the elk with water but more so a secure source of that water. If you cannot locate water in the timber, then look for the nearest sources along the fringes of the timber. If you locate a water source that is being used, i.e. lots of fresh tracks and murky looking water, then you can probably figure out how the elk are getting to it and follow the trail back to the bedding areas. You can also hunt the water source.

Bulls tend to bed up in the toughest, most rugged area they can find. My personal experience has shown that the older bulls seem to have some affinity for bedding up on or near steep slopes with a lot of vertical development, i.e. like a cliff or rock wall at their back. Perhaps they feel more secure thinking that their back is covered. Bulls often select a small bench that interrupts the slope to bed down on. This was exactly the case with the bull that I took in 2006. Cows are not as picky and will bed up almost anywhere. If you are looking for bulls and cows bedded together, look for the bulls to be bedded off to the side of the cows rather than mixed in with them. Focus your attention primarily on north facing slopes and in the most difficult to access real estate you can find if you're looking to bag a bull. Few elk hunters are successful hunting elk in their bedroom for a host of reasons but three big failing points are: 1) they do not manage their scent, 2) they move too fast, and 3) they are just not willing to put out the extreme amount of effort that this sort of hunting requires.

Q. "We'll be hunting southwest Colorado's 1st rifle season in the Powderhorn Primitive area. We have access at the far north end thru private property. Elevation will start at 8,400 ft. Not being able to scout the area other than 1 day prior to the opening how would you hunt the area?"

Steve, Louisiana

A. Hunt the dark timber. In all likelihood it will be warm during the day and the elk will have retreated to the coolness and security of the dark timber. Here they will remain from before sunrise to just before dark in the evening or later. This is the most challenging hunting of all.

Q. "Anyone know a good source on where to get maps that show boundaries distinguishing private property and national forest boundaries? I want to avoid trespassing and make sure landowners are not mislabeling their properties. I have an area in mind and would like to scout it after I can see a map of it."

Anonymous

A. BLM maps and National Forest maps are fairly accurate on such boundaries, but to really get down to it, county platte maps will show land ownership in detail. These maps are usually available to view at most county courthouses. Something to keep in mind when scouting or hunting, the law requires the hunter to know where the boundaries to private property are in the area he plans to hunt. While the maps give us information that was accurate at the time the map was surveyed, it may not be accurate when you are using it, as property boundaries can change from year to year. If you are hunting in close proximity to private property, it would be a good idea to try to arrange a visit with the landowners whose property boundaries might become an issue. If you are found on the wrong side of the fence, a map with old information may not be much of a defense if the landowner wants to press the issue. It is always better to be safe than sorry. Always ask.

Q. "We will be hunting in the south eastern section of Washington State this year. Last year we didn't have any luck due to the lack of knowledge and equipment. We have all of the areas mapped out and a game plan. We will be hunting dark timbered areas with water sources. My

question is: in order to get to these areas mapped it will require the use of ATVs. How far away should we stay from the area that we will be hunting with our Quads? Also what time should we get a start in the mornings to our hunting area? Note this is miles away from any roadways or hunting pressure."

Jeff, Washington

A. How far? Far enough that the elk in <u>any</u> area that you plan to hunt cannot hear you coming. This may be measured in miles depending upon the route you have to take to get into the area. On average I can usually hear an ATV coming a half mile away in mountainous terrain. (I don't really hear that well) Elk can hear far better, so I would consider a minimum of a mile from your closest point of approach. Take a look at your map and the area that you plan to hunt. See how close the road you plan to use comes to any part of your hunting area and avoid that boundary by at least a mile. Never cruise elk country on an ATV looking for elk. This is guaranteed to ruin not only your hunt but that of any other hunter in the area. In most cases elk are not acclimated to the sound of ATVs in their habitat. Therefore these sounds will tend to push the elk even farther away. Finally, it is important to take into account the impact that the sound of your ATV may have on the hunting of others in the area.

How early? If you are hunting in an area that is not heavily hunted, I would get going so as to have plenty of time to be in place where I want to hunt at least one good hour prior to sunrise. This gives things plenty of time to settle down after you get on your stand. It also allows you to better hear any elk nearby if they try to sneak past you as they move towards their bedding area. If there are significant numbers of other hunters around, you might want to try beating them to the top of the mountain so that they act as a driving force for you. This may require you getting going as much as two or more hours earlier.

Q. "I'm new to elk hunting and wondering how long to hang my elk. I've heard everything from 3 days to 14 days."

Pete, California

A. This answer applies to meat that is already out of the woods. A survey of chefs at better restaurants indicates that aging meat for 8 days produces a better taste. There is really no requirement to age the meat at all. If you do, make sure that it's in a cooler or similar environment.

Q. "I have been doing a lot of research on DIY bow elk hunts. Since bow season is usually early what tips should you use to save your meat if you are successful and are in a remote area?"

Anonymous

A. Here are the basics:

- Get your elk cooled down as quickly as possible. Bacteria can begin to grow as soon as the animal dies. Bacteria love warm moist environments to grow in, so don't give it to them. Usually this means getting the hide off pretty quick.

- While are your field dressing your animal make sure to remove any meat damaged by your arrow or bullet. This includes meat in the general area of the wound that has been spoiled by spilled blood. Once meat begins to spoil in one spot it can quickly move outward to surrounding tissue. Remove and discard any tissue that is questionable.

- If you cannot field dress your elk immediately and need to leave it, be sure to prop the cavity open after you have removed the entrails. This will allow air to get into the cavity and help cool the meat. If you have the time and are so inclined, consider boning out the meat as you field dress your animal. You can't eat the bones, they help to contain heat, and they are just extra weight you are going to have to pack out at the end of your hunt.

- Place each quarter in its own individual heavy duty game bag, seal the opening to prevent flies from getting in, and hang it in a tree in the shade. Make sure to hang it so that others critters cannot get to it. In most cases meat will be fine for a week if kept in a dark cooler area. The nighttime temps in elk country regardless of the time of year will cool the meat as long as it remains in good deep shade. Some folks like to pepper the quarters with black pepper to help keep the flies off.

Q. "What's the going rate to have your elk processed? I was surprised at the price they get in Craig for game processing. A man was telling me that they did a good job, but they charged him $250 for a cow elk and $125 for a deer this year. Here in Michigan the cost for deer is $50-$60. Now I know why I bring my meat home and process it myself."

Anonymous

A. Let me see if I can clear this up for you. Wild game processors work 24/7 during hunting season to process the deer and elk coming in the back door of their shops. Nearly every hunter wants his animal processed and ready to go before he leaves the area. That is understandable, I would too. This means that the processor may have less than 72 hours to process the animal, sometimes less than 24 hours. Keep in mind that the processor may have as many as 200 animals a day coming into his shop. The problem is that there just are not enough hours in the day to accomplish this monumental task, so the processor has to find a way to manage the volume. The way they do that is by charging a fee that discourages those who could and would probably do it themselves, and pays for the processor, his wife, his kids, and just about every able bodied friend he knows staying up 24 hours a day processing your game.

Processing game is not that hard, but a lot of folks would just as soon have someone else do it because they have better things to do with their time. Well guess what, so does the game processor, but instead he has chosen to go without meals, sleep and any measure of a normal life for about 6 weeks every fall, so that hunters like us can enjoy the luxury of continuing our hunt while he does the hard work.

Q. "I plan to hunt Colorado's first rifle season this year in a Wilderness Area at/near timberline near a series of high alpine lakes in south-central Colorado. I've been told by a few people that I don't need to go that high and likely won't see any elk at that elevation (11,000 feet+). Is that true? My primary motivation for choosing this location (other than appearing to be good elk habitat) is to escape the trucks, ATVs, and most other hunters. Obviously that

does me no good if there are no elk in the area. Any insight into high country elk hunting would be great. Many thanks!"

Kevin, Colorado

A. I would agree that elevation is not necessarily the key to locating elk. I would also ask, exactly what makes this area look like it would be good elk habitat. When pressed on this question, most folks really have no answer other than, "it looks like it." I guess that means that the area looks like something that they may have seen on TV or some DVD or video. My advice is that you not bet the farm on such an observation unless there are other key factors such as an abundance of new growth forage, water, and security for the elk present. Elk can remain high on the mountain if these factors that I have just mentioned are abundant. If not, they will travel to whatever place is required to find them. Your idea of avoiding ATVs and other hunters however is excellent. The farther you can get from both the better....if there are elk in the area as well.

Q. "OK, I have hunted for many years and you would think I would have answered these questions myself by now. For me and everyone reading, help me out here. With bull elk and the need to have four points on a side or a brow tine 5" or longer to be legal, what would be a general rule for a bino look measurement of the brow tine. I have always thought, if the tine passes the bull's nose, you're good. Would that be fair? Thanks"

Dave, Colorado

A. I'm not sure how others judge what five inches looks like, but I will compare the length of the brow tine to the length of an elk's ears. If it's a mature animal (not a calf) and the brow tine is as long as or longer than the length of an ear, I would consider the bull a shooter.

Q. "I feel dumb for asking this, but I'd rather feel dumb than not do it right. So the first thing you do when the elk goes down is to attach the carcass tag. But then you quarter it. So the carcass tag is on one of the quarters. I was wondering if this would be a problem when you are packing it out. What if a ranger stops you when you are packing out one of the three quarters that do not have the carcass tag on it? I know there is an easy answer to this, but I thought I would ask instead of worry."

KJ, Colorado

A. Great question! Place the carcass tag on the quarter that has evidence of sex attached to it.

Q. "Jay, this is our first elk hunt; we are hunting Colorado's first rifle season. You have been saying to hunt the dark timber and push them hard. What we have been trying to figure out is, do we split the three of us up or spread out to cover more ground, and try to hunt above 9,000 ft.?"

Anonymous

A. This question is a bit confusing, but I will give it a shot. Unless you have a particular spot such as a well used wallow or water hole that you plan to hunt, then you will want to cover as much ground as required in order to locate the elk. The best way to accomplish this task is to split up assigning each hunter a specific area that he or she is responsible for. This area assignment allows your group to cover more ground in a short time. An example of this might be that one hunter hunts the north side of a draw while another hunter hunts the south side. As you can see, you are still working as a team, but you are using the team more effectively. The tendency for new elk hunters is to hunt side by side. This has a number of disadvantages. First, there is a strong temptation to talk to one another...not good. Second, you both will be seeing essentially the same real estate...not good. Finally, if an animal pops up, now you have to choose who the shooter is. My suggestion, divide and conquer. The exception to this rule is when you are hunting with a young person and are using the hunt as a teaching experience.

Q. "We have hunted Baldy Mt. west of Pagosa Springs, Colorado for years with some success, but in the last two years we were unable to harvest an elk. We are going to try going up _ _ _ _ Rd east of _ _ _ _. (Deleted by author for obvious reasons) What do you suggest is the best way to find elk in the southern portion of the Weminuche Wilderness? We have never been there and don't know of anyone who has hunted there. I knew where to go look for fresh sign where we used to hunt for years. I am stressed out about trying to find sign within 3 days of the start of the first season. I'm thinking high elevation east and north facing slopes."

Scott, Texas

A. You and about 100,000 other elk hunters are asking this same question right now...less than two weeks before the rifle season opens. Unfortunately there is no quick solution to the problem of not knowing where the elk are. Only solid homework and time on the ground before the season can provide a reliable answer and this kind of preparation cannot be easily accomplished in three days prior to the opener of the season. Start planning your 2009 elk hunt the day you get home from your 2008 hunt. That being said, talk to locals and other hunters on their way out of camp about elk locations; hunting north facing slopes is a very good tactic; hunt the dark timber; elevation is not always a key.

Q. "We will be hunting the McClure Pass area in Colorado during the first rifle season. At what altitude should we expect to see bulls during this time of year?"

John, Minnesota

A. Unfortunately and honestly there is no hard and fast answer to this question. The only tip I can offer on hunting lines of elevation is that if a frost has occurred in the area recently, i.e. within a week of your hunt, then I suggest hunting just below the frost line as the forage will not have been burned below the frost line, leaving the forage more palatable to the elk. Elk do not inhabit specific elevations based upon the time of the year. While they do tend to stay higher on the mountain until forced down due to severe snows, there really is no general rule that I am aware of that says elk will be at 10,500 feet or 8,000feet, etc. on any particular day. If you or someone you know has hunted this same area in the past and you have located elk, then that is where I would start my search.

Q. "I will be hunting the southwest area of Colorado during the first week of November. Do calls work at this time of the year? What would a person do to have success?"

B. P, Wisconsin

A. I would refer you to previous Q&As on the subject of calling in this book. What would you do to have success? Honestly I have written four complete books on this subject, so you can see that the answer is a bit more complex that it may appear if you are new to elk hunting. Here are four tips to get you going: 1) Get really smart on elk. Elk hunting ain't deer hunting. How can you do that in short order, you cannot, but if you read books then I would suggest reading: Elk Hunting 101, Elk Hunting 201 and Elk Hunting 301, or any other good book on the subject…and there are lots. 2) Hunt all day every day you are in camp...no mid day back to camp breaks. You have to locate the elk and usually this requires you to cover a lot of ground, 6-10 miles per day and you cannot do this resting in camp. 3) Pay very close attention to your scent and the wind. Carbon based scent management clothing products will only work for about one day of elk hunting...two if you're lucky, after that they will become saturated with odors and will not provide any scent management advantage at all. You must know where the wind is all ALL times. The nose of an elk, even at long distances, is far more sensitive than that of a whitetail. 4) Hunt the dark timber (pine forests) north facing slopes most of the time. That should get you started.

Q. "How does snow affect elk? How much does it take to usually push them down and I assume they just hunker down during snow storms or will they actively feed if it's snowing? We scouted about a month ago in the West Elks Wilderness at about 11,500' we found lots of sign and couple nice 5x5's. There has been some snow lately but not more than a foot or so, do you think they would still be up there or should we get lower? Thanks!"

Ryan, Colorado

A. From a hunting perspective a foot of snow is a welcomed sight for a number of reasons.

- It is easier to visually locate the dark silhouette of an elk against the white backdrop of snow.
- You can spot elk tracks with a good set of binoculars from a mile away.
- The cooler weather that accompanies snow is helpful in keeping the elk moving more as they search for sources of food.

It takes quite a bit of snow to move elk out of their traditional summer range, as much as thirty inches or more in some cases. I've seen elk feed right on through a brief snow storm, but if a big one blows in, they will typically hold up until it blows through. Be ready to hunt immediately after the storm as the elk will start to leave the timber pretty quickly. A month can be a long time in elk country. You might have a look at the 11,500' area you scouted earlier for fresh sign, but don't hold your breath. Elk are continually on the move seeking food and security during hunting season. With the high numbers of hunters that invade the Colorado high country each hunting season, there is a good chance that the elk may have moved.

Q. "I've read your first three books and gotten a lot of benefit from studying them - thank you. My hunting party is headed on a guided hunt this fall in South Central Colorado. Just a couple of final questions for our preparation: How can we best support our guide's efforts? Are there particular things that we should do (or not do) that will make their jobs easier and more likely to

get us into the elk? What should we budget for meat processing expenses (yes, I'm confident, we've been preparing like mad)? With respect to gratuity for the guides, is there a standard that we should consider? Thank you."

A. McDonald, Wisconsin

A. Listen to your guides. They are there to help you succeed. In most cases the guide knows far more about elk hunting, particularly in his area, than the hunter. When their hunter harvests an elk it really makes their day. If you have questions about how your guide plans to hunt, ask him before you head up the trail to camp. If you have concerns about your guide's qualifications, talk to the outfitter (owner) immediately. If you have experience calling elk, tell your guide while in camp. If he needs your help in this area he will tell you. If he says to leave the call in camp or in your day pack, do it. In most cases the guide will set a pace that is a bit outside of your comfort zone. That's ok. You should adjust to keep up with him. If on the other hand the guide continuously runs up mountains like a goat, you need to explain to him that you need to slow things down a bit. Pacing yourself to last the entire hunt is very important. Be prepared for a lot of physical discomfort and dealing with it. Elk hunting is one of the most physically challenging types of hunting in the lower 48. Make sure that you and your gear are in 100% working order.

Consider your guide to be your hunting partner, not your nanny. You and he, or she, are a team. Each of you have a responsibility to perform, so make sure you do your part. Every day is going to be long and arduous so I would encourage you to get as much rest as possible. Some folks like to sit up into the wee hours talking and socializing. While this is a part of elk camp, do it in moderation. You will be getting up early and three or four hours of sleep will start to adversely impact your hunt very quickly. Make sure you bring good earplugs. There is almost always some guy who snores like a freight train in camp and this will definitely affect your rest if you have trouble sleeping. Never leave home without them. If you happen to be that guy, do everything you can to minimize the racket you make at night.

Meat processing in the local area averages about $250 per animal. During the hunting season the meat processors are working 24/7 with elk and deer coming in the back door continuously. It may take as much as three days to get your meat back. In some cases the outfitter can have the meat packed back down the mountain and taken to the processor while your group continues to hunt.

Gratuity is very important: Ten percent of the cost of your hunt is the customary amount. So if you paid $5000 for the hunt, then $500 would be a good tip. Gratuities for guides are similar to those for waiters in a restaurant. If they provide good service i.e. they do their job and work hard then a good tip is in order. Tips should not be dependent on your success or harvest, only on the actual performance of the guide. Camp cooks usually get a tip as well. This can run anywhere from $25-$100 depending upon your view of their performance. Keep in mind that food in elk camp is usually not like eating at home or in a restaurant so be sure to set realistic expectations in this area. While some camp cooks are excellent chefs, quantity sometimes wins out over quality.

Q. "Is there a specific cow call that produces better than others? I had an experience this season where I was calling for a friend and when I used a certain call the bull would respond better. I'm just wondering if this is just bull specific or if certain calls have been proven better than others."

Dean, Wyoming

A. Honestly in almost 25 years of elk hunting I have not found any single call that consistently gets responses from elk more frequently than another call in every situation, i.e. the 'killer silver bullet elk call.' Anyone who is selling elk calls will tell you that their call is the best call on the market. That is how they attempt to sell elk calls. As you correctly state however, sometimes one call will work better than another on a specific bull or cow. Calling elk is a lot like talking up another person. If one approach doesn't work keep trying until you find the approach (call and calling sequences) that do work. Often times it is more often a case of how you use the call, i.e. the calling sequences and when you use it, more than the actual sounds that the call puts out. I carry four or five calls with me all the time, including mouth diaphragm calls, open and closed reed calls, squeeze type calls and a bugle. Many times hunters new to calling elk err by calling too much and failing to be aggressive and move in on the elk when the elk hangs up. Try using a variety of calls and calling techniques. If the elk fails to come in; check the wind, make a plan, and make your move.

Q. "We are hoping to get in pretty deep, and are wondering if anyone knows of a packing service. We will be on foot but were hoping that we might be able to hire

someone to pack out an animal if we are blessed to be successful. Can you recommend someone?"

Anonymous, Colorado

A. The packing out of game is considered by the Colorado Division of Wildlife to be an 'Outfitter's Service'. This means that in Colorado, only licensed outfitters can provide this service on public lands. You may run into any number of individuals who will offer to provide this service to you for a fee. Make sure you see a copy of their outfitter's license or at least get their outfitter's registration number and all contact information before parting with your cash. If you by chance engage someone for this service who is not a licensed outfitter in Colorado, you could end up with a very hefty fine and possibly the loss of your animal and your gear. An alternative would be to rent horses or mules and do it yourself. A caution here is to only elect this option if someone in your party is thoroughly familiar with the care of these animals. Otherwise the stock could easily become more of a liability than an asset.

Q. "I need some help with suggestions on ways to transport elk meat home. Coolers work fine, but what if you have more elk than coolers?"

Anonymous

A. If you lay a plastic tarp down in the bed of your pickup, next lay out a fully opened sleeping bag (you can even use two), followed by another layer of plastic tarp. Place the meat in the center and then repeat the process in reverse....plastic, sleeping bags, plastic, securing all the corners for an "airtight" fit. This works exceptionally well for processed and frozen meats as the insulated meat stays completely frozen for a two-day trip home.

One year we had taken two elk in for processing and the evening before we were to leave, we got another elk. We brought that elk home quartered and surrounded by the frozen processed meat. The quarters were cold and hard to the touch as if they had been hung in a walk-in cooler. For those who wish to use dry ice or even regular block ice, just wrap either in a garbage bag or other plastic, as you probably do with an ice chest. I can tell you that once you try this, you will never pack ice chests again for the purpose of caring for meat. Thanks to Tom from California for this great tip.

Q. "I will be hunting elk in Colorado this November. I will be using a scope that is 5X15X40mm with a mil/dot reticle. My intent is to do range finding with the scope. The scope is a Bushnell Legend. It did not come with any mil/dot spacing or power that should you be used for range finding. I plan on calibrating the range using a vertically placed stick with size marking on it at 100, 200 & 400 yards. My Nosler reloading book tells me that the back to brisket spacing can range from 32 to 35 inches, while Hartt Wixom tells me in his book 24 inches. Is Nosler talking Washington elk and Wixom Colorado elk? What is the number I should use for Colorado?"

Ron, Ohio

A. Rather than jump through hoops estimating the size of a bull or cows back to brisket measurement, and then attempting some sort of mathematical calculation for range based on this assumption, I would suggest you invest in a good rangefinder. This will give you the exact range, in mere seconds, without the added problems of the math. Once you know the range, then apply the appropriate hold over from your ballistic tables and take the shot. I sight my elk rifle in to shoot dead on at 250 yards. I know that if the bull shows up at 100 yards and I place the cross-hairs dead on, I will hit 2.0 inches high. I can live with that. If the bull shows up at 300 yards I hold over 2.8 inches, and for 400 yards, I need to hold over by 12.3 inches. Of course all of these numbers are based on a level shot. If you are shooting up or down hill you will need to apply a correction. Many of the newer rangefinders like my Bushnell Scout 1000 with ARC can make this angular correction for you.

Q. "I have heard the terms "summer range" and "winter range" used with regard to where elk live. Can you define what these terms mean?"

Jeff, Colorado

A. In most, but not all, cases, elk inhabit different geographic areas in summer and early fall than they inhabit during winter and early spring. This is primarily due to the difficulty of acquiring enough quality forage during the winter and early spring months when the snow levels are at their highest. In general geographic terms these areas, i.e. summer range and winter range, have been historically mapped and can be found online by searching the website for that particular state's Game and Fish or DNR agency. In addition there are a few commercial entities that can provide you with this information as well.

Q. "I've been elk hunting for a few years now, and it's a lot different from the stand hunting I'm used to when we hunt whitetails at home. Using the still hunting method, at what pace do you walk? Is it 3 steps and stop and look? I'm guessing you look as far ahead as you can?"

David, Missouri

A. First let me state that every hunter is going to hunt at a pace that is comfortable and works for him/her. That being said, I have found that the slower I go, the more elk I see. And I see a lot. If I am hunting open ground or in and out of cover I may not stop at all until I am ready to do some glassing. In most cases under these circumstances, this means that I will move 50-100 yards and stop.

When I am hunting dark timber I change my entire strategy including my pace. Consider this. The average man's stride is about 36 inches or three feet in length. When at rest and glassing or studying the area before you, you want to focus and try to see everything from your nine o'clock position to your three o'clock position. Look behind, below, above and through every tree, bush, and blown down timber looking for some small patch of color that seems out of place or that small insignificant movement that may clue you in to the presence of hidden elk. If you step forward one step, just three feet, the relationship between your eye and everything you just looked at has changed and you see a new and different view or perspective. Moving one step at a time, studying the environment, and then repeating is my best suggestion for moving through dark or heavy timber. Most folks either cannot or will not do this and they move way too fast. The result, the elk detect you first and they move out leaving the hunter with no clue that they were there.

Q." I recently read your book *Elk Hunting 101* and found it interesting how you said that the older you get the less you want to carry. I agree and don't want to carry seven knives to field dress an elk. What type of knife is best for

field dressing elk conveniently? I also plan on quartering the elk and packing it out on my back. Let me know what you think."

A novice elk hunter

A. You will find that there is very little that is convenient about field dressing an elk, especially if you have to do it alone. That being said, I carry two knives. One is a drop-point fixed-blade Buck Vanguard that is an old favorite of mine, and the other is a Benchmade Model 551 folding drop-point knife. Each knife has its strengths and having two in my daypack allows me to work longer between sharpening. I also carry a small ceramic 'V' sharpener and a folding diamond dust sharpener in my daypack. When it comes to good knives for field dressing elk, there are many excellent name brand products on the market. I avoid the cheaper imported knives as the steel in these is often inferior and can break leaving you with a real problem and no solution miles from a trailhead.

When field dressing game as large and tough as elk having a sharp blade is critical. When I am preparing my gear for elk camp I use a Lansky sharpening system to get the blades to 100%. One of the keys to getting the sharpest edge possible on a blade is a consistent angle between the blade and the sharpening surface. This is where a Lansky really shines. I take the Lansky to camp, but I do not carry it in my day pack.

When you are field dressing your elk, try to avoid allowing the blade of your knife to come into contact with the hair on the hide any more than is absolutely necessary as this will dull your blade fast. For packing out, I suggest boning out the meat before you load it up. The bones are just added weight that has virtually no value so why carry them?

Q. "What is the best color combination for fletching arrows? The colors should be ones that are not noticeable to an elk at close range, but would still make an arrow easy to find."

Patrick K, Washington

A. Your argument about easy to find is the same argument that most of us make when it comes to fletching or vane color. I use easy to see wraps as well as easy to see vanes. Not only does this make them easier to find at the range or if you miss while hunting, but these are also easier to track visually immediately after release. To worry about the color of your arrow vanes with regard to how the elk might or might not respond to them would probably be splitting hairs. I wouldn't worry about the color.

Q. "I hunt elk in lower elevations between 7,000 to 8,500 feet in south-central Colorado. The terrain doesn't have tall pines, aspens, or slides. How would you locate bull elk there in mid November?"

Jake, Colorado

A. The specific area that you are hunting is pretty much a high desert environment. Cover is predominantly PJ (Piñon Juniper) and sage. Your best bet will be to find a high point and spend a lot of time with your binoculars or spotting scope glassing for the elk. You might try some cow calling, but the sound of the call may not carry far enough in the area you are hunting. Also look for hidden water sources that the elk may be hitting.

Q. "Being an old geezer and still trying to bag my first elk on a DIY hunt, what is your recommendation for the best

season to harvest an elk? I have hunted Muzzleloader season, and this year hunted the last two weeks of archery. I definitely saw more elk this year and had a ball, but I was unable to put meat on the pole. I lost a good bull due to a poor shot placement. Put another way, when would a hunter have the highest odds of getting close to elk on public land?"

Mike, Pennsylvania

A. I've not found that there is a best season. I have personal preferences and those depend upon where I'm hunting and what my expectations are for the hunt. By this I mean, do I want to have a bowhunting experience? If so, I hunt near the peak of the rut when bulls are bugling like crazy. If I am meat hunting, I usually plan for a late season cow hunt and look for an area that has a migration. If I want to hunt a really nice bull, i.e. 300+ B&C, then I will usually hunt private land during 3rd rifle season in Colorado or New Mexico. As you can see there really isn't a short answer to your question.

However with that being said, for the average hunter, hunting the first available rifle season following or near the tail end of the rut is usually a pretty good time to have a good chance of sneaking up on a raghorn bull as they are younger and can sometimes still be found hanging around the cows. Their youthfulness sometimes works to the hunters' advantage as these bulls can sometimes be located using a cow call. If I cannot hunt this season, then I jump to a rifle season where I can expect that there will be some measure of snow on the ground. This makes it easier to locate the elk and the elk tend to move around a bit more once the weather has cooled off.

Q. "I will be hunting the late-late hunt (1st weekend in December) with a rifle in very rugged terrain. This area will have been hunted the prior week. I recently injured my knee and will not be able to hike the canyons as I had originally planned. This hunting area is at about the 4000 to 5000 foot elevation and gets some elk migrating through to their winter range as well as some that stay all winter. Usually there is no snow yet at this elevation so it is hard to determine where they will be moving. I plan to glass from elevations and then to cow and calf call hoping to get a bull to come to me. My question: Do I have a better chance of getting a bull to come down to investigate my calls or do I have a better chance of having one come up from below? Do I hunt from above canyons or from below canyons and does this seem like a reasonable approach considering my new physical limitations?"

Mike, Arizona

A. The general consensus among our researchers is that elk more readily respond to calls from below than from above. This does not mean that elk will not come uphill to a call, just that more seem to come in when the caller is below or on the same level. On that note, I would not bet the farm on getting bulls to come into calls that late in the season. It may happen if you get the attention of a younger bull but in my experience, it's not likely. By that time mature bulls have lost interest in breeding and are lying low and recuperating from the rigors of the rut and often ignore calling.

Is this a reasonable approach? I would have a couple of concerns given your stated physical limitations. If you plan to hunt migrating elk, they will likely be on the move. Once you locate them, you may have to relocate and perhaps quickly to get into position for a shot. How do you plan to do this? If you kill a bull, how do you plan to get it out considering the bad knee? I ask these questions to offer a suggestion. Consider hunting with at least one hunting partner, possibly two who are sensitive to your limitations and are willing to help you by doing more than their share of the work. Also, you should have a serious talk with your physician about your hunting plans and see what they recommend. I really hate missing out on an elk hunting season but it beats the heck out of getting oneself into a situation where there is no good way out.

Q. "I've been thinking of trying a decoy this year. Do you feel it helps bring elk into bow range? I usually hunt solo & have elk hang up at 65-70 yards a lot."

Anonymous

A. Many times a well placed decoy can make all the difference between success and failure in elk hunting. Bowhunting is a short-range game and the list of frustrated bowhunters who have seen their hunt fall apart when they could not get a bull to come into range or close the distance themselves is long. When a bull hears your cow elk siren's song or your bugle and decides to move closer and investigate, there usually comes a point where he wants to see who or what is making all the ruckus. While some bulls are either so fired up or so stupid that they will close the distance without hesitation, many wary bulls and hang up just inside that magic hundred yard mark looking for the source of the call. I've seen this time and time again. The bull will come in from hundreds of yard away and then just stop and stand dead still 65-90 yards away looking and waiting.

In some cases this can last as long as ten minutes which can fry the nerves of even the most skilled hunter. This is where a good well-placed decoy can make all the difference in the outcome of your hunt.

Another case where a decoy can make the difference is when you are hunting open range with little cover such as sage or PJ— Piñon-juniper— flats. Getting a bull to come in across all that open terrain can be a challenge. Here a good decoy placed where the bull can see it may do the trick. I have a great bowhunter friend who occasionally uses a decoy to hide behind as he sneaks across such open areas to close the distance to a difficult bull.

Q. "Took a friend and new hunter out 4th season looking for a cow. We ended up finding elk in some PJ areas. This place was dry as a bone and I got to thinking about how often elk need to water. The nearest obvious water source in the area was a river about 1 1/2 miles away. Has anyone ever read anything concerning the water requirements for elk? Most places that I've hunted elk previously have had numerous water sources."

Anonymous

A. The general consensus is that proximity to a good water source is far more crucial to elk than the amount of water they intake. As a rule elk prefer to remain within a half mile of a good water source at the most. A third of a mile is even better. If elk cannot access water within this distance they tend to move on to another area with a more local water source. This does not mean that you cannot find elk in such a waterless environment, just that they probably will not stay there for long. Hunting near such a well-used water source can be productive if you make sure that the wind is in your favor.

Q. "For heating the tent with a wood stove at night, I have heard that coal heats better than wood? How different is it, and how much does it normally cost?"

Anonymous

A. Coal heats very well. Make sure to clean your stack out daily. A fellow elk hunter states that it will cost you about $40 bucks for ten days worth of coal. Two large chunks on the embers and you are set for the night. Anthracite coal is best but bituminous   coal   will   do.

Q. "This year's hunt was a mid-season trip where it rained with a full moon. The elk were not talking at all unless you count 3:00 AM. They were bedding around 4:00AM and not getting out till after 10:00PM. How do you crack this nut? I have run into this more than once and nothing I have tried has worked. How do ya get them when they get like this?"

Anonymous

A. Hunt during mid day. Unless you are hunting private land and are afraid of pushing the elk off of the ranch, there is really no reason not to hunt the elk while they are bedded. It is very hard hunting and in my estimation about one in 50 elk hunters has what it takes to pull this type of hunt off, and only one in 500 will even try it, but given your experience it looks like you do not have much to lose. Elk hunting is an exercise in persistence and endurance. I bet I have said this ten thousand times to one elk hunter or another and until you have successfully brought an elk to ground, you will not fully understand the truth of it.

Q. "I'm about to buy a new wall tent for the upcoming season. Can you make any recommendations?"

Anonymous

A. Davis Tent and Awning and Montana Tents each have a very long history of making quality products. I've not owned a Montana, but I have owned a Davis tent and it never failed. Reliable Tents and Tipis out of Billings, Montana is also an excellent product. I would encourage spending a few extra bucks if that is what it takes. You do not want to have your tent fail and ruin your hunt.

Here is something to keep in mind. Canvas wall tents require a specific level of care during the hunt (see more on this in my book, *Elk Hunting 201*) and before you put it away for the season. If you fail to follow the instructions, you could damage the tent. If you will be hunting when there is standing snow or ice, be sure to bring along a good plastic tarp to put over the top of the tent. If snow or ice stands on the top for too long, nothing will keep it out.

NEVER, EVER treat a canvas wall tent with waterproofing. It will ruin the tent. If you have questions on this, just call the folks at Davis Tent and Awning in Denver, Colorado.

Buy the fire-retardant and mildew-retardant canvas. It costs more, but will pay for itself in the long run.

If you have a wood stove in the tent, make sure to take the stove pipe off every day or so at camp and clean out the soot.

This will prevent a buildup which will cause the smoke to back up in your tent. Also make sure to have a spark arrestor on top of the stack. This will help to keep from burning the tent down during the night.

Q. "Lookin' for a good cheap fire starter. Got any ideas?"

Anonymous

A. Here are a few that work well and won't break the bank.

1. Cotton balls coated in Vaseline

2. Dryer lint, right out of the dryer or saturated with wax.

3. Trioxane fuel bars, better known as heat tabs

4. Steel wool and a Nine volt battery

Q. "If all goes well and I down an elk I want to make sure I have enough cooler space to get it back to town but I don't want to overdo it. How many coolers do you bring with to get your elk back to town?"

A. If you bone your elk out, one 150 quart cooler should do it, two maybe if it is a large bull. Keep in mind it will be heavy so watch your back when you get ready to load it up.

Q. "Just wondered if there is ever any trouble with theft or vandals around camp while you are out hunting during the day. We seem to be taking lots of stuff with us to make our week of hunting as comfortable as possible and wondered if we need to be locking everything up as we head out of camp in the mornings. I would like to think that everyone else is just another good ole boy like myself and is there to have a good time but you never know."

A. I've hunted elk for over 20 years and never had a problem with anyone walking off with gear left in camp. That said I also never leave any high dollar gear lying around in plain sight either. I keep all weapons and stuff like GPS secured when away   from   camp.

Q. "Can anyone tell me where I can find a topo map with satellite overlay?"

A. You can purchase these at www.mytopo.com. I have worked with the great folks at MyTopo for years and have never been disappointed with their products or service. You can order these products as well as conventional topo maps and aerial photos online. All products come in a variety of sizes and can be ordered printed on conventional paper, waterproof paper or laminated. Give them a call and ask for Kevin or Paige.

Q. "Has anyone ever bought a pair of hunting boots that they are completely satisfied with? If so, please let me know. I have had several different brands of boots in the past and have had problems with most. I really need a good waterproof boot that is comfortable enough to walk several miles a day. Thanks for any info."

A. Danner is #1 for me. I have hunted with them for years. These are some of the most comfortable and wear resistant boots out there. Hunting, hiking, fishing etc... I really like them. The leather/cordura is soft, very strong and very quiet compared to the other materials used now days. The support around my ankle with Danner boots is also excellent.

When you are in the store trying on boots make sure to wear socks that are the same thickness as those you plan to hunt in. Also it doesn't hurt to allow at least three-fourths of an inch of extra room between your big toe and the inside tip of the boot.

When you are walking around in the store testing the fit of the boots, try to find a downhill grade to walk on, the steeper the better. This will help you determine if your toe will strike the front of the boot going downhill. If your big toe touches the inside front of the boot, try the next size larger.

I always buy insulated waterproof boots. How much insulation you choose will depend upon your individual preference. If you hunt in fair to warmer weather, you may be able to get by with uninsulated boots; however I have found that 400-600 grams of Thinsulate works for all but the most extreme weather in the high country. Keep in mind that any boot, if not properly cared for, will fail. This means prepping your boot before you head out and cleaning them up after you get home.

Q. "Any tips on how to avoid Altitude Sickness in the high country?"

A. The following are tips supplied by hunters like yourself. They are not intended to be interpreted as medical advice. Always consult your personal physician first.

- A slow ascent is one way to prevent altitude sickness, but this may not be practical if you're flying direct to Denver International Airport. Still, try to give your body a break and take it easy once you land. If possible try to spend a couple of extra days in camp acclimating before you try any serious physical exertion. This means pretty much sitting around doing nothing.
- Stay hydrated. Doctors seem to agree that acclimatization is often accompanied by fluid loss, so you need to drink lots of water to remain properly hydrated (at least 3-4 quarts per day).

- Shelve the low carb diet. Melissa Gallagher, founder of Healthy Being, LLC says "A carb-rich diet is key because carbohydrates naturally replace muscle glycogen levels and prevent protein from being burned as energy." She adds that high-carb diets also require less oxygen for metabolism and digestion.

- Gingko is reported to enhance circulation, which means more blood gets to your brain and to your extremities. More blood means more oxygen, which is how some researchers think gingko helps alleviate the affects of thinner air. Mark Rosenberg, M.D. says, "The best way to protect yourself from altitude sickness is to begin taking 60 mg of gingko each day at least five days before your ascent. Studies show its effective just one day before, but five days provides even better results. He recommends using a gingko extract rather than a capsule-generally liquids absorb into your body better."

- Listen to your body. You don't need me tell you that rest and sleep will help you adjust to the elevation. That sluggish, exhausted feeling? Those drooping eyelids and dragging feet? That's your body's way of telling you to get some shut eye – probably the most helpful thing you can do.

Q. "Not knowing what the road will be like where I am hunting, what are the chances I will need to use tire chains? I have one set, I believe this is all that is required. Would it be wise to have another set to use on all four tires? Do people usually use them because of the snow or just because of the rugged terrain? Just trying to figure out if chains are something I should expect to use or are they

something I will just carry with me for insurance if the weather turns bad?"

A. Just like they say, you can never have too much insurance; likewise you can never have too many tire chains. Weather and road conditions in the high country can change quickly. There is no substitute for a set of four well-fitting tire chains for each vehicle. Also consider taking a good tow strap and a come-along or winch. The latter two only come into play if you get high-centered or a have a wheel off the road, but roads that were 100% bone dry when you drove in during the early pre-dawn hours can become slick, muddy or impassible in just a few hours if a storm blows through your hunting area. You might want to include a high lift jack as well.

Q. "I'm flying out for my hunt. Any thoughts on how to get my meat back without breaking the bank?"

Anonymous, TX

A. When you get your elk, try to get it in to get processed and tell them to sharp freeze it. Usually they will do a quick turnaround for nonresident hunters. (1 day) Have a couple of large coolers with duct tape handy. Wrap the heck out of the coolers with the tape. Check them as baggage. (Anything over 50# gets charged extra - check with your airline) Just be sure that the meat ALWAYS stays with your flight. A boned out cow is about 110-150 pounds of meat.

Q. "Hey guys, me and a buddy are planning an elk hunting trip this year and we will be camping in a tent and I was wondering what you guys who camp do to prevent bears from becoming uninvited guests? If you put a cooler with food inside the bed of your truck with a camper shell

on it, is that going to be enough to keep a bear out of it? What about the trash from your campsite, what needs to be done to keep bears away? Any tips and advice you could give to a total newbie will be greatly appreciated."

A. The best way to deal with bears and other uninvited guests is to avoid attracting them in the first place. Bears are attracted to food more than anything, so do everything you can to minimize the smell of food when you cook and eat. Put a lid on every pot or cook food covered with foil in the coals of a fire. As soon as you're through eating, clean up the camp, wash all the dishes and make sure all food is in tightly closed containers. Never dump out grease or leftovers and if you're the one who has cooked, change your clothes and put them in a plastic bag.

Also a big problem I have seen with inexperienced campers is they like to throw trash in the fire. Thinking that the fire will destroy the trash and you won't have to worry about throwing it out. When you do this you are burning the old fish you caught or the beans you ate or leftover steak bones and whatever it is you ate. What happens is all that stuff makes a very delicious scent that the bears can pick up for miles and miles. Be careful what you try to burn while camping.

Situate your sleeping site, whether it's a tent or just a bedroll, several yards away from where you cooked and eat. Don't camp near a running stream, as tempting as it may be. Avoid berry patches and obvious game trails when you set up camp, too. By setting up on these you are inviting wild animals who are coming to their own food source to investigate a new one.

Don't wander off alone; always stay with a group of people and in the daylight hours, make some noise. That will warn wildlife that you're in the area and reduce the chance of a surprise meeting, or of finding yourself between a momma bear and her cub - a very dangerous situation. If you find yourself in this dire situation do not turn and run as you will only be chased down. Stand up and slowly back away. Never go near that cuddly cute little teddy bear of a cub, his mom is sure to be lurking somewhere nearby.

If attacked by a black bear the rule is to fight back like your life depends upon it. It does. If however, you are in Grizzly country and attacked by a griz, the rule is draw your knees and elbows into a ball placing your interlocked hands behind your neck, roll over and play dead no matter what happens. Generally if a grizzly attacks it will break off the attack once you are no longer considered a threat. In this case you are just trying to survive the attack.

Use common sense, don't be overly fearful, but don't be overly brave, either. Most wild creatures don't want to deal with you any more than you want to deal with them. Enjoy the wilderness camping, hunting, fishing, and all that the outdoors has to offer.

Q. "I've been hunting the high country for years using a good wood stove for heat in my wall tent at night. Recently I thought about switching to using a propane heater. Anyone got any thoughts on this?"

John, Wyoming

A. Once upon a time, when I thought the ability to endure pain and discomfort made me more of a man, I heated with a wood stove on those bone numbing high country nights near timberline. Then one day the elk-hunting fairy-god-mother said, "Jay why don't you try a radiant propane heater." So I says to myself, "self ... why didn't you think of that? But, not getting up at 2AM to pee and stoke the fire in subzero temps ain't manly." So again I say to myself "manly schmanly, I like staying warm...all night." So I did two things, I quit drinking anything after dinner and I bought a 3-burner propane radiant heater that can crank out up to 45,000 BTUs (spelled butt toasting units...really British Thermal Units). The first time I used it, I lit off all three burners right before we all hit the sack in my 14x16 Davis wall tent. Within an hour all six of us were sweating, so I backed it off to one burner set to a Medium temp range. Everyone slept like babies all night and awoke to a nice toasty tent the following morning.

Here is something to keep in mind if you decide to go the propane radiant heater route. It needs oxygen to burn so make sure to leave the flap where a wood stove stack would exit the tent open to allow fresh air to vent in. This also leaves a way for exhaled CO2 to get out which is a major contributor to the condensation found on the inside of a tent that is sealed up. If you place the heater near the stack opening it will help to warm the cold air descending from the opening.

I used this heater for many years. In fact I still have it and when I find myself back in the high country in a tent, the propane heater will right there with me. Guys this is a no brainer. One bottle of propane like the one you use on your BBQ grill at home will provide adequate heat for about 3-4 days if you run it on one burner all night. If you need a second bottle to make it through the week, take an extra one.

Q. "Both times I have hunted; we drove maybe a mile or two from camp, parked the truck and then hunted from there. We saw very little, and only brought home one doe

among both hunts. I'm starting to wonder if we should be making a more concerted effort to get further away from our camp site, especially with the smells and noise associated with camp. In my first hunt we hunted relatively close to the roads/4x4 trails. Granted, we were all a little out of shape, and not completely prepared for a lot of hiking, let alone packing out an animal, if we had harvested one. But we are doing our best to prepare now for next year's hunt, planning camp sites and planning on camping there during the summer months to scout and check out the area more. Once you have set up camp in the high country, how far away from camp do you go to start the hunt in the morning? Do you drive for x-amount of miles then hike in from there, all before sunrise, or what? I also don't want to make a mistake by setting camp too close to a good spot, and driving the animals away from us.

I'd like to get a feel for what I need to prepare for, and so I can get my buddies mentally and physically prepared for it --ahead of time. Those 7-P's of planning tell me I have a lot to do, but its December. I think it's better to start planning now, than to decide two days before hunting season how far out we're going to go."

Anonymous, CO

A. Keep in mind that 80% of all elk hunters hunt within one mile of some sort of road. If you want to avoid all of this excess hunting pressure, you will have to have the will and ability to move beyond them.

Don't park the truck directly across the road from where you plan to enter the timber. There are many road hunters out there that just cruise forest service roads looking for where other hunters are going in to hunt. They will pull up right behind your truck and may possibly head into the timber right behind you. Once you locate the spot where you plan to enter the timber, drive past it some distance, park, unload, and walk back. If you want to keep where you are entering the timber a secret, don't use flagging tape to mark the spot, every other hunter knows what this means. Arrange a few branches on the ground in a way that only you will recognize or better yet, enter that spot into your GPS

I would approach your hunting area(s) like this. First find the areas you want to hunt - you will definitely want more than two or three good spots within that area. The elk move a lot and sooner or later they will be where you are. Once you find a good area, then find a place to camp, somewhere nearby. A mile or two is within reason. Any more than that and you are wasting time driving instead of walking to your hunting spots. Do not let easy road access dictate where you hunt.

Look for some spots where there are no road spurs off the main road. Patches of timber just off the road from these areas can hold elk. Look for a wide spot in the road and pull over and hunt. A lot of hunters drive by these areas.

It's a good idea to be where you want to shoot well before daylight. Settle in, get comfy and let the morning wake up around you. You will be surprised how many times you forget that you are hunting.

Try to get in the best shape as you can - you don't have to go on steroids - just try to get the legs & lungs working. When you go up to scout, push yourself a little to see how you are doing - wear a pack with at least ten pounds of weight in it and carry a heavier stick or staff. When you are hunting you will be wearing a pack and carrying a weapon. A 1-2 mile hike to your "honey hole" is not uncommon. That means a minimum of 2-4 miles for a morning hunt, 4-8 miles if you get lucky and shoot something.

Q. "I am trying to put together a hunt with some buddies from back east in about two years. I have a few locations that I am thinking about and wanted to get some info from you all. If we looked at having someone pack us in to a destination that was 3-5 miles from the trailhead drop us off with our own gear and then pick us back up and pack out any elk what kind of a cost would we be looking at? There would probably be three or four of us on the trip."

A. Drop camps can be excellent ways to get back in far enough to get into less pressured elk. If you're hunting Colorado, be sure to use only a licensed outfitter, otherwise you could risk a hefty fine as this service is defined by the Colorado Department of Regulatory Agencies as an outfitter service and is illegal on public land for anyone other than a licensed outfitter to provide.

Drop camps can include a completely outfitted camp including tents, wood stoves, cooking gear and more. These typically run anywhere from $1500 - $2500 (2009). Just pack-in services average $100 - $150 per horse per day. You should plan on paying for the time of the wrangler as well. This can run from $100 - $150 per day.

Q. "During first rifle season this year, I was working a faint game trial along the bank of a stream, which was bordered by black timber, hunting my way back to camp. I was hoping to catch something coming to the water,

which heavy tracks suggested was occurring. With only about 15 minutes of shooting light remaining that day, I was sitting on a blowdown (across the game trail on the bank of the stream) on the edge of the timber, marking a route back to camp on my GPS. After setting my GPS to route me back to camp, I took a good look in the direction I had been heading (downstream / downtrail), and not seeing anything, slowly stood up to continue my hunt. As soon as I reached my full height, I heard a crash right behind me, and watched a 150 lb lion take off across the creek bed. He stopped at about 40 yards, took a good look at me, and then disappeared at full speed. After watching him disappear, I surveyed the area behind me, and found the tracks where he had been walking down the trail and jumped off the trail and into the creek bed. The tracks where he jumped were slightly less than 5 yards from where I was sitting (behind me).

This being my first "close encounter" with a mountain lion, I have two questions:

1. Do you think this was a chance encounter, that he was working the same trial I was, hunting the stream, and he just happened to run into me? Or am I just lucky......

2. What do you do while in lion country to protect yourself from a lion attack?"

A. In over 20 years of elk hunting and hiking the high country I have never had such an up close encounter with any predator. I say this to give readers some idea of how rare such an encounter is. That being said, the smart hunter is always aware of his surroundings when in the back country. If you are using a cow call and hunkered down out of plain sight, this would be one of those times as the call acts as advertisement to all the game in the area including elk, lion, bears, and wolves. If you are in the open the animals will have a chance to see you earlier and should avoid you.

Most such encounters occur when man and beast run into each other unexpectedly as was probably the case in your encounter. Humans are not in the lion's food chain. Attacks that do happen other than by accident are usually committed out of ignorance by adolescent males or older cats that can no longer bring down game like elk and deer. Sometimes the critter doesn't realize its mistake until hunter and beast are engaged. In this case, fight back, make yourself as big as possible, and make a lot of noise. The only exception to this rule that I am aware of is if attacked by a grizzly. In such a case the experts say, to ball up, protect the back of your neck and play dead until the bear decides that you are no longer a threat and leaves the area. Experts also suggest remaining in this protective position for some time to ensure the bear has left the area; otherwise you could provoke another attack.

Q. "I was hunting in southern Colorado during the last two weeks of the archery season. I have hunted this area for several years and have always had luck getting onto the elk. However this year the elk were extremely quiet and would not answer any calls (cow/bugle). My question is this, what do you do when the elk are quiet? How do you get them engaged and what do you do when they leave the area?"

Mike, PA.

A. Most likely, the elk have in fact left the area that you are hunting in. Elk are continually on the move seeking out sources of high-value nourishment especially when winter is close. It is their #1 priority! Elk are pretty vocal critters, especially the cows. If you are not hearing cow talk OR if you cannot locate fresh sign (translated POOP) in the area, then I would suggest that they have relocated.

What are your options? 1) Try hunting nearby drainages. Elk will only go as far as they have to in order to locate a new food supply. That is a long hump you may say. Yes it can be, but hunting where there are no elk is the alternative. One thing you can do right now is to start getting yourself in the right mindset of "do whatever it takes and go wherever you have to in order to locate the elk." This can require a great deal of personal discipline, more than some hunters have. It's up to the hunter to determine what he or she is willing to commit to in order to be successful in their elk hunting. 2) (long shot if your hunt is only a week long) You could try waiting it out in the area you had planned to hunt to see if another group of elk move in...Remember the elk are always moving. Think of it as a game of musical chairs. Elk Group A moves to chair # 2 while Elk Group B moves into Group A's recently vacated chair (area) #1. If Group B does not find a promising food source in that area they will move on to another area as well. Herd dynamics with regard to finding good sources of food are very fluid and in a continual cycle.

What can you do to engage silent elk? There is no silver bullet here...and believe me everyone is looking for one. In my opinion there is very little you can do in such a situation. Some will tell you to call differently or mix up your calling in an effort to stimulate elk talk. If elk are in the area and go silent there is usually a very good reason, the immediate perceived threat posed by predators.

This is not rocket science. Put yourself in their place. You are in the woods. You know that there are critters roaming those woods who want to do you harm. How much noise are you going to make that may give away your location? In situations such as this getting elk to talk has, in my 20 plus years of elk hunting, proven to be a real challenge until the threat either goes away or the elk relocate to an area where the threat is less.

Here is one thing you might try however. Mama elk have a very tough time ignoring the sound of what they think may be a stray calf. You might try some limited calf calling. The key here is not to call too much in any one area or they will catch on. You have to sound like one lone lost calf trying to relocate the herd. I have tested this on cows more than once and in many cases a lone calf call can get a cow to either respond vocally or quietly come in to see what is going on. The sound of a lone calf, I believe, tugs on a part of that momma cow's intellect that she finds difficult to ignore.

Q. "I will be hunting the first rifle season in the Flat Tops Wilderness Area in Colorado. This will be my 3rd year hunting this particular season and area. I have read a lot of postings that say you need to hunt the Black Timber during the day on North or East facing slopes. My problem is that the black timber is so full of blow downs and debris in this area that it is virtually impossible to navigate through there quietly, no matter how slow you go. I feel as though I am just chasing elk out of the area I am hunting as no other hunters get off their ATVs and do any walking. With so much ATV traffic and impenetrable timber, how would you suggest our hunting group hunt this terrain?"

Nate, Colorado

A. You are not going to like this answer but hunting that dark timber is still your best bet. It is just about the toughest hunting there is, but when the ATVs are all over the place, which can be the case on public land, this is the one place where the elk can find security, food, and water. If you feel like you are making a lot of noise, use a cow call from time to time. Elk make noise moving through the dark timber also. The call may help to settle the elk down as well as you. You are going to have to move extremely slowly. This will help you in a couple of ways. One...you make less noise. Two...You take more time checking out every single tree and piece of brush before you take the next step. Three...you will not tire as easily.

Q. "What's the best technique for getting to those pre-planned spots during the predawn (still dark) hours? It would seem flashlights would be too ... 'flashy' and easily seen by those nocturnal elk from a long ways away."

Mike, Colorado

A. In many cases if you give your eyes a few minutes to adjust to the darkness you will be surprised at how well you can see to navigate with just moonlight. Some folks think they cannot do this, but give it a try. Just take it slow at first. You will be surprised at how fast your eyes will adjust. This is always the first option. If this fails to work for you or if there is no moonlight at all, try using a small flashlight or headlamp with a red lens. Neither deer nor elk see well in the spectrum of light that includes red. The use of the red lens cover will also help to preserve your night vision.

Another tip is to leave early enough that you don't have to rush. If you have already scouted out the area you are heading to, you can also use reflective tacks that can be placed on trees to help you find your way in. These are about 1/2 inch across and help to define a path with little more than moonlight. Remember to place the markers on the side of the tree that will be facing you as you walk to your hunting area.

Q. What are the most popular Binoculars under $500 for Elk hunting? Also what power binocular is the most popular?

Joe, PA.

A. Some of the more popular elk hunting binoculars for under $500 (MSRP) include: Alpen Apex 10x42, Nikon 10x42 Monarch ATB, Leupold 10x42 Cascade, Bushnell 10.5x45 Infinity, and Vortex 10x42 Fury.

10x40 and 8x40 seem to be among the most sought after configurations as these offer a fairly wide field of view with adequate magnification. Keep in mind that as you increase the power of magnification you will decrease the effective field of view, which can mean more work for the hunter. I tell folks to never go cheap on optics whether it is your riflescope, your spotting scope or your binoculars. Quality glass (binoculars) that you can use continuously for long periods of time without getting eye strain can make or break your elk hunt. Spot and stalk is, in most cases, the preferred method of hunting elk. This requires the hunter to spend a lot of time (hours) each day with his eyes in the glass. Lower costing optics will give you severe eye strain and headaches. This results in the hunter not spending as much time glassing as he should which often results in a less successful hunt.

Q. "I have data from biologist, game commission, and environmental researchers on elk summer range concentrations. Will the elk be in these areas during bow season assuming they are undisturbed? Is all of this research bull?"

LA Harris, KY

A. Seems to me like you have asked the right folks. As a general rule these individuals and agencies really do want to help hunters. I would give some serious consideration to their answers. Is this research "bull"...absolutely not. That being said, in any agency there will those whose research is more thorough than others but overall they do a very good job.

Elk generally remain in their summer range as long as they have access to quality forage. Keep in mind that elk will move a lot (translates many miles) throughout this range in order to find food and once hunting season begins to avoid contact with hunters. It usually takes a lot of snow to motivate elk to begin their migration to winter grounds and in some cases they will only move lower down the mountain staying in the same general area all winter.

Q. "I am shopping for a spotting scope for an upcoming elk hunt. I also hunt deer, antelope, etc. so I want one that is good for all species. Do you prefer straight or angled? What about power? I am looking at both 18-36x60 and 20-60x80. I will be hiking in so I want something that is reasonably light."

Kevin, CA

A. If I plan on glassing for hours and hours I use a 20-60x80 spotting scope with an angled eyepiece. It's much easier on the neck. The trick is to set yourself up to be comfortable for long periods of time. If you expect to be glassing slopes that are miles off, then a scope with high magnification can make a lot of difference when it comes to telling if the bull you are glassing is one that you want to put a stalk on. Usually when I am hunting I take either a smaller scope with a straight eyepiece or more often I just use my binoculars. You can buy some good lightweight tripods and use an adapter to attach your binoculars to it. This is my preferred method as it cuts down on excess weight in my daypack. I use Alpen Ranier 10x42 binoculars and they do the job for anything but extremely long distance spotting.

Q. "I am planning a Colorado elk hunt and am looking specifically at a GMU near Grand Junction. I would love to combo with a mule deer, if possible, but my primary focus will be elk. I am interested in your thoughts related to which gun season (muzzleloader or rifle) would be best for elk and why? Also, which season would give me the best opportunity at both an elk and mule deer combo? I would love to go during muzzleloading but am not sure if my job will allow for it."

Mike, NY

A. Many hunters coming west for a big game hunt want to get as much bang as possible for the buck, i.e. hunting elk and mulies at the same time and who can blame them. There are pros and cons to this strategy. Let's look at the pros first. Both mule deer and elk are found in abundance in many western states. 1) The area around Grand Junction has plenty of both.

2) The cost of a mule deer tag is around $300 (2009 prices) so while this is not cheap, it won't break the bank. 3) Having the extra deer tag in your pocket in the event you run across a buck during the course of your elk hunt provides you with double the chances of bringing something home.

Now let's look briefly at the cons. 1) Elk range and mule deer range can overlap, this overlap can be as small as 10-20 percent depending upon the amount of available food for each respective species. Hence if you are in primary elk habitat there may not be many deer around or vice versa. 2) Here is what usually happens. The hunter not having luck at locating elk early on switches his efforts to locating mule deer. He gives this a day or so and if he does not have luck he then switches back to elk. The end of the hunt comes much too quickly and the hunter looks back and wishes he had stayed focused on his primary game animal for the entire hunt. **Solution:** If your bank account can handle the cost of the extra tag (all deer tags are draw) then by all means buy one and put it in your pocket "just in case." But remember to keep your focus on elk hunting, if that was your primary target.

Colorado's muzzleloader season overlaps the archery season in mid September and can be a truly awesome time to hunt as the bulls are approaching the rut and can be very vocal. This vocalization helps the hunter locate the elk. If you can draw a tag (required) this is a great time to hunt. If you elect to hunt rifle and want to pursue both deer and elk you will want to plan to hunt either the 2nd or 3rd combined season. You can hunt the 4th season but this is a limited deer/elk season.

Q. "I have only hunted elk once and that was via a drop camp. I have finally recovered from that endeavor (Florida

boy, smile) and would like to try again. What hunt, muzzleloader or late archery, would most likely yield the greatest possibility of peak rut activity? I plan to enter the draw and need advice on how to proceed."

David, Florida

A. It is important to keep in mind that the peak of the rut can vary somewhat. Timing of the rut, i.e. when a particular bull's mating switch gets turned on is determined by a specific level of testosterone in his brain. This level begins rising as early as mid August, but the trigger event is determined by photo period. This is the day/night, or cycle and frequency of darkness/light entering the bull's brain via his retina. In general, the peak of the rut falls later on the calendar the farther south you go. This is due to the angle of the sun and how that angle changes at any given geographic point as one moves towards or away from the Equator. While elk in northern Colorado may peak in mid-September, those in southern Colorado will likely not peak until later in September. Colorado's muzzleloader season (2009) runs Sept 12-20. Given that most modern day inline muzzleloaders have an effective range of 100-150 yards I would consider hunting this season in the northern half of the state for your best opportunity to connect with that bull. If you prefer to bowhunt, look toward the last week in September and the southern half of the state for peak rut activity.

There are many other factors that could factor into the success of your hunt, but since this will be only your second hunt and I'm guessing that you will not have the opportunity to scout much ahead of time, this might be a better bet. Now here is where your previous hunt experience will put you far ahead of those who are hunting for the first time, you know how challenging your hunt will be physically...they don't. Now is the time to start getting into shape. I hate working out and running as much or more than the next guy, but those who are the most successful are usually those who either know where the elk are beforehand OR those who are prepared to hunt long and hard...this would be you.

Q. "I hunt the Grant Mesa National Forest, and this is my 2nd year hunting the area. My question is for the first week of archery season, I find that there is not a lot of vocalization going on at this time. What is a good method of locating or type of calling is there?"

Jeffrey, WV

A. The short answer is that many bulls, especially older bulls are not ready to start talking this early. Younger bulls sometimes begin testing out their pipes early often because they don't know any better and they are mimicking what they hear from other young bulls. Bugling in elk is a form of male advertisement. Until a bull's testosterone level reaches a certain point in his brain, he doesn't know that he has anything or any reason to advertise. Vocalization generally increases as a bull approaches the rut. In west-central Colorado this usually occurs in mid-late September. Cow calling is often the preferred method of locating elk as they vocalize all year long. By calling to the cows and listening for a response the hunter is hoping to determine where the elk are in his area. Then the hunter wants to move to a point where he may be able to glass the cows to see if there happens to be a bull(s) in the area that he wants to pursue.

Q. "My question is regarding ground blinds. I have hunter buddies of mine who tell me that hunting from a

ground blind is a no-no in elk country because the woods are the elk's "living room" and unless a ground blind was left to sit in the woods for a few months it would scare more elk away than anything. What are your thoughts?"

Joey, CO

A. As a rule I like to spot and stalk elk, however if you find a location that the elk are frequenting quite a bit like a wallow or water hole, a ground blind may be an option.

According to Brooks Johnson founder of Double Bull Archery, a light-weight shoot-in-any-direction ground blind like their MatriX 360 blind can be a very effective tool for hunting open areas that offer no concealment from the eyes of curious cows. If you are trying to put a stalk on a good herd bull, Brooks offers that the challenge is not in outsmarting the bull, it is in not getting busted by a couple of dozen sets of eyes surrounding the bull. If you can locate a water hole or wallow ahead of time, a ground blind placed within shooting range may be your ticket to success next season.

While I have hunted deer and turkey from natural ground blinds successfully for years, the concept of hunting from a portable blind like Double Bull's MatriX 360 for elk brought a few questions to mind that I wanted to ask of one of the leaders in this industry. First and foremost I wanted to know how long it takes elk to acclimate to the presence of such a ground blind. Since elk seasons in some states can be quite limited, as short as five days in some cases, a drawn out acclimation period could be the kiss of death for the hunter who must travel long distances to hunt and is faced with a limited season. Brooks indicated that unlike deer which do have to get used to the presence of a blind, field tests in Montana on elk demonstrate that even in open areas elk will readily walk right past a newly erected ground blind that was not there the day before with little if any regard.

My second question to Brooks concerned how well the blind might help to mask a hunter's scent. Brooks responded that in cases where the wind was allowed to blow through the blind towards the elk, that whatever scent emanated from the hunter would in fact be carried on towards the elk. He quickly countered however, with the recommendation that he makes to all who ask, that Double Bull Archery recommend that no more than 180 degrees of the shooting windows of such a blind be opened at any one time, less if possible. I drew from this response that all one would need to do to prevent one's scent from being blown down wind would be to close off the upwind windows. On the MatriX 360, Brooks told me that all shooting ports open and close with a Silent Slide mechanism. If an animal circles behind the blind, and you have that side of the Surround Sight™ window system closed, you can simply open one of the four (4) silent "just-in-case" shooting ports on that half of the blind in order to get the shot without detection.

A tip from the folks at Double Bull Archery for helping to manage scent is to cut some fresh sage stems or pine boughs depending up whether your blind is set up in the open flats or in the edge of timber, and lay them over the top of the blind. These freshly cut branches will emit odorous oils that will help to mask scent inside the blind.

Q. "What grain broadhead should a person use on a elk? Is a 1" cutting diameter 4-blade broadhead too small? How much kinetic energy is a person looking for? How many yards should a person expect to shoot?"

Troy, Wisconsin

A. You've asked several common questions about archery hunting for elk. I have asked my good friend Roger Medley, a champion archer and great bowhunter to respond.

What grain broadhead should a person use on elk? The correct answer is whatever broadhead will tune the best. I've spoken to many who will practice with a 100gr broadhead and then switch to a 125gr head right before season in an attempt to add that extra little bit of kinetic energy. There a several bad outcomes when doing this. 1. A 25gr change in arrow weight will only result in a kinetic energy change of about 4/10th of 1 foot/pound. The second, and more detrimental outcome, is that by increasing the point weight you may now have an under spined arrow, thus resulting in erratic arrow flight and possibly a wounded animal.

Is a 1" cutting diameter 4 blade broadhead too small for elk? In short, the answer is no. One thing to remember is that the cutting diameter is different than the cutting surface. While the broadhead may produce a 1" diameter cut it actually can produce 2" of surface cut due to the total cutting surface.

How much kinetic energy is a person looking for? Here is a list of what seems to be the general consensus. Remember, nothing is better than a well placed shot.

Small Sized Game - 25 ft-lbs

Medium Sized Game (Deer, antelope, etc.) - 25-40 ft-lbs

Large Sized Game (Elk, Moose, Black Bear) - 50-65 ft-lbs

Dangerous/Tough Game (Cape Buffalo, Grizzly, etc.) - 65 ft-lbs and above

If you'd like to know what kinetic energy your setup is producing you can check out our website.

http://backcountrybowhunting.com/articles/tools.php

How many yards should a person expect to shoot? My suggestion is be comfortable out to 60 yards. However, most shots are taken at less than 20 yards.

Q. "After sighting in my bow with fieldpoints my broadheads are not landing where my field points are. Should I adjust my pins?"

Anonymous

A. No. When you were growing up, did you ever put your arm out of the car window tilting it up and down and feeling the effect of the wind on your hand? The airflow over a broadhead, especially the larger bladed ones, has the same effect on arrow flight. If the arrow leaves the bow slightly point down the arrow will land lower in the target than an arrow with a fieldpoint. Mechanical and smaller bladed broadheads were designed to help alleviate the effect of a poorly tuned bow.

To properly tune your bow with broadheads, and after sighting in with fieldpoints, start by shooting a fieldpoint arrow and a broadhead arrow at 20 yards to compare the POI (point of impact) difference between the two - make a note. Then move to 30 yards and make another comparison. Work your way out to 60 yards noting the differences between the fieldpoint and broadhead arrows. If your broadheads are consistently landing lower than your field points your arrows are coming out of your bow slightly point down. Move your rest in the direction you want your broadheads to move, in this case, to bring the broadheads up adjust the rest up. Make these adjustments in very small increments, 1/32nd of an inch at a time and shoot again. At 60 yards this can produce a POI change of several inches for the arrows with broadheads and no change for the fieldpoint arrows. Keep making this adjustment until your fieldpoints and broadheads are impacting the target together and you'll be ready to go.

Q. "I have been hunting elk for eight years and I have been filling at least one tag for each of the last four years. I picked up archery hunting two years ago and killed my first elk with a bow last year. I hunt all public land. My question is how do I find bigger bulls. I've killed small bulls and one big one. My biggest bull to date is about 250. I spend over fifty days a year chasing elk. I think that I should being seeing more trophy bulls. Am I doing something wrong? I am young still (20 years old). Is the reason I don't see too many big bulls because there are only a handful of them on public land? Are people shooting elk to young? I thought Colorado fixed that when they put an antler restriction on some units. What do I do? I want to be a guide some day, and if I can't find big bulls I probably won't have too many clients."

Brandon, Colorado

A. If I got it right you are 20 years old. You have probably heard this more times that you would like. Be patient and do your homework. We live in a world where folks, especially younger folks, have become accustomed to quick results and if they can't have it, they look for shortcuts. If you're looking to whack a 300+ bull, short of pure dumb luck, you will have to work at it and take whatever time is required. Also, if you really want to harvest a 300+ bull, you have to develop the discipline to pass on younger bulls. This is tough regardless of how old you are, but trophy hunting means that one has to be willing to go home empty handed some years.

Big bulls did not get to be big bulls (6 or more years old) by being stupid and easy to locate. **First you will want to hunt in an area that is known to have bigger bulls in it.** This requires homework much of which can be done from home. In CO, that is usually means hunting limited entry units which require preference points or private land, so start applying for points and save them up. You don't have to have 15 Preference Points, but 5-6 will help a lot.

Second, hunt areas that are way off the beaten path and scout these areas as much as possible in the summer. Think of it this way. If more than a handful of other hunters can get there, they will and this will either kill off the older bulls or run them into hiding. Being 20 years old here is a big asset as you should have more energy and stamina to get to and hunt these difficult to access areas than older hunters. Believe me, in 20 years you are not going to want to go into these areas either. How far is far enough? I suggest a minimum of four miles from ANY road. Hunt from a spike camp so you don't spend so much time going back and forth to a base camp. In most cases that is just wasted time and energy. Even better, hunt with your camp packed on your back. When you locate a shooter bull, drop the pack and plan your stalk. If at the end of the day, you are still searching, set up a small cold camp. This means no fire or cooking of any kind. A Bivy sack and sleeping bag will do in most cases. In the morning, load up and head out in search of that elusive bull again.

Say you have a week to hunt. I would plan a route that looks a bit like a horseshoe on a map. This allows you to cover a lot of ground and gets you back near to where you started by the end of the week.

Finally, what is a big bull. Most folks say 300 B&C is the lower end of that threshold. There are lots of 300-class bulls in CO, believe me. Hunting big bulls, i.e. herd bulls, with a bow is very challenging. Your chances are about 25% of what a rifle hunter's chances are and his (if he is real good) on public land to score on a big 300 or better bull in Colorado are less than 10%. This should give you some perspective.

If you want to be a guide, talk to some outfitters. They are easy to find and usually looking for young fresh hard working meat...I meant to say guides. If you have the basics down, they will teach you the rest. They will teach you their areas. The work is hard, days are long, and the pay is cheap...$150 per day usually (plus tips).

JAY'S SUMMARY

You are probably going to think, why didn't he just put this up front and save me the trouble of having to read through all of the information that came before. If I had, you would have missed a wealth of information, some of which might be the nugget that makes the difference between success and failure on some future elk hunt.

I have literally talked with thousands of elk hunters and those who are considering elk hunting for the first time. For those new to this adventure, somewhere in the conversation I get the feeling that they want me to hand them a Silver Bullet, that if used will provide them with a shortcut to a successful elk hunt. Folks, not only do I not have one, I don't know of anyone who does. And I know a lot of successful elk hunters. How do consistently successful elk hunters do as well as they do? They make a point of gaining a thorough understanding of elk and then they religiously apply some basic principles over and over again. Elk hunting is like anything else. The more you practice, the better you get. It's not rocket science.

If you take the following suggestions to heart, you will go into elk country armed with about a 75% advantage over the hunter who does not.

- IF YOU GET IN SHAPE, YOU SHOULD BE ABLE TO GO THE DISTANCE REQUIRED TO GET INTO ELK. IF YOU DON'T, BE PREPARED FOR SOME PAIN AND DISAPPOINTMENT.
- GET SMART ON ELK HABITS AND BEHAVIOR. THERE IS NO SUBSTITUTE FOR A GOOD

WORKING KNOWLEDGE OF HOW ELK LIVE AND WHY THEY DO WHAT THEY DO.

- HUNT WHERE THERE ARE ELK. IF THERE IS NO FRESH SIGN, THERE ARE PROBABLY NO ELK IN YOUR AREA TODAY. HUNT ELSEWHERE. RETURN TO THE AREA ANOTHER DAY.
- BE PREPARED TO WALK AS MUCH AS 10 MILES EVERY DAY.
- LEARN HOW TO USE A VARIETY OF ELK CALLS WELL. KNOW WHEN TO USE THEM AND WHEN NOT TO. PRACTICE LISTENING TO ACTUAL ELK SOUNDS ON A TAPE OR CD. RATHER THAN FOCUSING ON CALLING ELK IN, USE THE CALL AS A LOCATOR, BE AGGRESSIVE AND PLAN A STALK..
- MANAGE YOUR SCENT 100% OF THE TIME. ALWAYS KNOW WHERE THE WIND IS, AND USE IT TO YOUR ADVANTAGE.
- BE DEADLY PROFECIENT WITH YOUR WEAPON OF CHOICE AND KNOW YOUR CAPABILITES AS WELL AS YOUR LIMITATIONS.
- GET VERY GOOD AT JUDGING DISTANCE OR PURCHASE A GOOD RANGE FINDER. MORE ELK ARE MISSED OR WOUNDED BECAUSE OF POOR RANGING SKILLS.
- EAT WELL AND HYDRATE OFTEN. YOUR BODY USES HUGE AMOUNTS OF FUEL IN ELK COUNTRY AND IT HAS TO BE REPLACED.
- TAKE YOUR TIME, GO SLOWER.
- NEVER HUNT ALONE AND ALWAYS TELL SOMEONE WHERE YOU ARE HUNTING.

Passing It On

As one who has been blessed with much in life, I find myself in a place where giving back has come to mean more and more with each passing year. I had not planned on including any hunter's stories in this volume however, when the following story of a young girl and her hunt came across my desk recently, folks, I just lost it. After reading Raelynn's story through a couple of times, I was convinced that in sharing her hunt with you, her words might touch a place in your own heart and perhaps you might pick up the phone and ask a young person to go hunting with you. Here is the story of Raelynn Northup, in her own words.

A Daughter and a Hunt a Dad Would Be Proud Of

Since I was three years old I had always wanted to go hunting with my dad. Then six years later he was gone. I never got to go hunting with him. I pretty much just wanted to give up on everything. My dad was my everything. I was a total daddy's girl and I did not know what to do because he was gone. Then it got to me that God wanted him. Now he will be in a better place and now he will be with me every second of everyday. I lived everyday as it came and now its three years later, I'm sitting in my room and I hear my mom calling my name. She asked me if I want to go on this hunt with Mark Stackhouse. I said of course. I was so excited. It's only a couple months till the hunt and we go down to Woodland Park to practice. I was very nervous. I was scared that I would shoot bad and about the kick of the gun. We get there, and there were a lot of boys and I wanted to prove to them all that girls can do better than boys. So I got up to shoot the gun and freaked out for no reason. I pulled the trigger. It wasn't so hard at all . I shot a couple rounds and as I fired my last round, I got the one and only bull's-eye. I was shocked.

Days and days go by and it is finally five days till the hunt. I was so excited that I went and got all my stuff together that day. I wanted to leave right then but I still had to wait. It's Friday and we wake up at 6:30 AM and start with the very long drive to get there. We got to Woodland Park and then we were on our way to meet Randy at his house. Mark and I meet him and the other kid and his dad then head to Colorado Springs to meet the rest of the kids at McDonald's. We meet all the boys, eat dinner, and then head out to the hunting place. It's a long drive and I slept the whole way. When I woke up we were there. We meet all the other boys. Then I got scared and remembered that I was the only girl. But kept a smile on my face cause I like being around boys better than girls. We walked into the building. Wow it was freezing.

I meet our host Donny, then Randy starts talking about how trust is the most important thing and we all need to trust each other. It hit me that I have to trust everyone, so I put all my trust on every single person in the room. Afterwards I was tired so I went to bed and opened my eyes and it's time to hunt. My heart was beating so fast. I was so nervous to go but at the same time so so excited. We get to the spot where Donny told us to go, we sat in the car for a couple minutes and then Mark saw deer. It was crazy. The deer were right there and we just got there. Mark and I get out of the car quietly. Mark told me to watch were I walked so I did not step on a branch or anything and make noise and scare the deer. We walked and got to a spot where I could have taken the shot, well I thought I could have taken the shot, I was so ready. I wanted to get one so bad. Mark said no I could not take the shot 'cause it was 300 yards, too far. We kept walking and walking, and we could not find the deer. So we go looking some more. We walk up this hill thing and it was crazy steep and I had the gun and slipped. I didn't fall but was close to dropping the gun, but Mark grabbed it. More and more walking and we found a dead porcupine. It was kinda sad. We sit down for a while and Mark was on a walkie-talkie with Randy. He pushed some deer towards us. I was sitting there looking, and then I see deer running. I was excited so I told Mark loudly. The deer were running, and ran up towards a house. Dang, we met up with Randy and one of the kids and his dad. We go did not find any deer so we went back for lunch.

We see that someone got a deer. It was Matt (I think that is his name). I was pretty disappointed because I really wanted to get the first deer to prove to all the boys that girls were better. I watch them skin the deer. Matt kinda looked like he was scared to get blood on him. Then Randy says it's time for the father son lunch. I was pretty nervous about this because Mark is not my dad and I really didn't know what to say. It's been a long time since I had a guy to talk to, and it was awkward. Mark started talking about choices and how that is how you make yourself, by all the choices you make. That totally made me think, and ya duh Raelynn, it is. We talked more and then walked back to the camp. When I got back I learned that one of the boys got a deer. He was so proud, the smile on his face made me smile. Now I was even more ready to get a deer. I grabbed my gun and license and headed out with Donny, Mark and a kid and his dad. We get in the truck and just started driving and they found some deer. We get out of the truck and were in a hurry to get closer to the deer. We got closer. I got the gun set up to shoot, my heart was beating so fast it felt like 100 miles per hour. I shoot, oh dang I missed. A couple minutes later I hear Donny say that there they are, I get set up again and now it feels like my heart is beating 200 miles per hour. I take the shot, the deer made a weird movement and then I was so excited and proud.

We went to go find the deer that I shot and it is nowhere to be found. Then Mark points out blood. We follow the blood and it keeps going for a very long time then all of a sudden stops. We looked everywhere and could not find the wounded deer. We saw lots of other deer but none of them where limping or anything. Wow, I totally felt like I just wanted to break down and cry because, I knew that once you wounded a deer your hunt was over. Now it is getting dark and we head back to camp and to Donny's rules which are, if you miss he gets to cut a piece out of your shirt. There I was and I missed twice, he cut one piece from the front and one piece from the back. It made me laugh and I went and changed into a pink shirt. But that is what Donny really wanted, he wanted a piece of my pink shirt. We start talking about tomorrow and Randy and Donny were deciding whether I get to go back out in the morning and they decided yes. That made my day, they are the nicest people I have ever met. I went to sleep excited to get up and try again on getting a deer. I go to sleep and bam, the next day is here. It was freezing cold, I wake up, put on my warm stuff, head to the big living room, and get some hot chocolate which puts a little heat in me. Mark and I go out and we see lots of deer with horns but could not find any deer without horns and by then it was snowing like a blizzard outside. I totally lost my hope, and tried to still keep my head up high. Mark gets a message on his answering machine saying to meet Donny back at camp if I have not got anything yet, so we went back to camp. Once we got back to camp everyone else has gotten their animals and are cleaning up and then getting ready to leave. Donny, Mark, and I head out to go find me a deer with no horns. We look at several different places, no deer to be seen. Then we drove out to a place that took kinda long to get to. We found deer and I start yelling when I see them which I should have been quiet, but I was so excited. I did not get out of the truck fast enough, and then the deer heard us and ran away. Then we drive a little more and find some. More of the adrenaline in me was running so fast, so very fast. I get the gun set up to shoot and aim it right at its shoulder while it's snowing. Bang, I shoot the gun and got the deer! OH YES! Right when I shot that deer, I thought of my dad and how proud he is up in Heaven watching. We go up to the deer and then I got sad. It was still alive moving its head. I had paralyzed the deer. Then Donny asked me if I wanted to shoot it right in the shoulder so it would not have to suffer. BANG....that deer is dead! We take pictures and then drag my deer through the snow, over the fence, and to the back of Donny's amazing truck. Donny tells me how proud he is of me and gives me a hug and the same with Mark. If it wasn't for Mark and Donny I would of never gotten my deer. They are two amazing guys and I'm glad I have them in my life.

On the way back it totally hit me, it's not all about getting the first deer, duh me. It's about the people you meet, the memories you make, and the love that comes out. Now then I was glad every single thing happened because it was meant to happen and sure enough made it the best time ever. I haven't been really into God ever since my dad died. It's taken me this long to figure out it happened because it was meant to happen, to put my daddy in a better place and from that day on God has been more in my heart than he ever has been.

We get back to camp to gut the deer. Wow, I never knew how gross that was, but I dealt with it. We loaded up our stuff, the deer in the back, and it was time to say goodbye to that amazing place. It was sad saying goodbye to Donny and Randy, I didn't want to leave, it all felt like it was over way too soon. Donny now has a place in my heart. I thank Mark with all of my heart for taking me. Now I hope I get to come back and hunt on this every year. It's a great memory that is going to last forever.

Raelynn Northup

Tips from Elk Hunters

Shooting Sticks: I'm trying to stay within a budget for next year's elk hunt so instead of buying those expensive flimsy chop sticks...I took two 3/4" diagonal 6'6"long pieces of bamboo that I found while out hog hunting one morning, and tied them together with some nylon line I had laying around to make my own chop sticks. It also doubles as a sturdy light weight walking stick.

Sleeping Bag Warmth: Whenever I'm out hunting in cold weather overnight I will carry a few hand warmers with me to toss in the sleeping bag...you will be surprised how well it works. Also, for sleeping in a cold tent, a knit stocking cap is the next best thing to heat.

Online Scouting: Figured out your area to hunt? Pull it up on Google maps. You can switch between the topo map and satellite image to see what the area 'really' looks like. We didn't take any of these with us, but wish we had! Missed one meadow we wanted to hit.

Cyber scoutin' is great and a fun way to pass time between seasons.

Avoid the Pain: Cut those toe nails and finger nails. The toe nails get long and when not cut will cause pain while walking any distance as well as cutting through those expensive socks. A good haircut can also help to make the head gear fit better too.

Tag Placement: I have found that using a baby pin for your tag and placing the tag on the inside of the ear works so easy and simple. You can take it on and off in seconds. No rope or string to use. More secure, too. Use a small hole-puncher for the month and date you have to cut out. It only takes a second and is a heck of a lot easier than using a knife.

Clean Up: I am sure everyone has a way or secret to cleaning the hard blood and out from under fingernails etc. after cleaning your game unless you wear rubber gloves. I have found over the years that grape juice works wonders. I use a rag soaked in grape juice and also pour some over the hands. Within a couple minutes all is bright and clean. At camp, use the scent free soap and all is done.

Preparing For The Shot: Most people think they are better shots than they really are in the field. I have seen guys that can shoot repeatable groups that are sub half-inch from the bench, but cannot hit a pie plate when shooting offhand. Take a little time at least every month and get some range time. Once your gun is sighted in, stay away from the bench rests. Shoot from field positions, sitting, kneeling, prone, and offhand. Shoot from shooting sticks or get used to shooting from them. It will greatly improve your accuracy in the field. A fun exercise is to run back from the target to the shooting position and while you are still huffing and puffing, try to keep the shots in a paper plate sized target. If you are on a public range, be the last one back during the cease fire and shoot as soon as safely possible.

Tent Repair: If you need to repair a half dollar size tear or smaller I found that using Lock Tights Stick n' Seal product works well. I've used this method for the past couple of years and this stuff is bulletproof. Just wet the finger, apply resin to finger and smear over hole. If it's bigger than that I used iron on fabric that you can buy from the Wal-Mart fabric section. Cut the piece about an inch wider than the tear, get creative with the iron and heat up the tent fabric. Don't use an iron on nylon or other synthetics. As a precaution apply Lock Tight (Stick n seal) to the edges and it should hold for several years.

Knife Sharpening: Most people over sharpen their knives. Once a good edge is established it is not necessary to sharpen it again on a stone unless there is some real damage to the edge. All that over sharpening reduces the useful life of the knife. Usually, a touch up with a good steel will straighten out the edge and the knife will be sharp again without grinding it away. When the steel will not bring the edge back, it is then time to hit the stones.

Another hunter writes: I used to use a stone but I could never get it to work for me. I'm too inconsistent at holding the angle correctly. I switched to a electric sharpener and it really worked a lot better. Then from time to time run it over a steel to keep the edge aligned. Now I have all my knives so sharp they scare me. Yes, they are that sharp. It's expensive but worth every penny.

Boot Care: I bought a pair of waterproof Cabelas Outfitter boots ten years ago for bear hunting and every year I coat them with a layer of Snow seal. First I clean the boots with a damp cloth and wipe the Snow seal generously all over the boots. Next I will take a hair dryer and melt the Snow seal on the boots. By doing that the heat will open up the pores of the leather and absorb the Snow seal. It keeps the leather from rotting and preserves it for years and years.

Hunter #2: You're so right. I only do one additional thing. I put a good amount more on the seams, toe and tongue. I then use a lighter to melt it into the leather. I will do this three times and also brush the boot between layers. I tell you this, if a boot will leak, it will be at the seam, toe and tongue. After doing this for years and years, my full leather Danner boots are soft and the tread will be gone before the leather. I would rather re-tread the boot than buy another pair when that day comes.

Long Range Shooting: The ballistics books, charts, and software programs are great at giving you an idea of the downrange bullet path, wind drift, and retained energy, but the shooter really needs to verify what is happening with *their setup* on paper before heading afield. Each gun and ammo combination can give a different velocity reading, even if they are identical guns. Differences in bore sizes, chamber dimensions, barrel length, throat erosion, etc. has an effect on velocity. Different weather conditions can mess with velocity also. A load that is tested in the hot summer months may lose 5% of its velocity when used in sub freezing temps of winter. Do yourself a favor and verify at long range what is actually going to happen before you float the crosshairs over the bulls back at 450 yards.

Another issue is wind deflection. Guessing the holdover with today's laser rangefinders is not extremely difficult. Knowing how far to hold into the wind is where the real long range shooter is separated from the close range plinkers. Even shooting the latest greatest fire breathing Super-duper-splat-em magnum is going to be affected by the wind. Taking a 400 yard shot with just a 10 mph crosswind will result in just over 9" of wind deflection. Add 9" to the group size under hunting conditions, and you can see how easy it is to turn a heart/lung shot into a gut shot. Bottom line is, know the ballistics for your setup. The wind is the spoiler of good groups. Since its almost always varying in direction and velocity, it's difficult to guess where the bullet will fall downrange. On long range shots the wind direction can be blowing different directions at the same time due to terrain variances.

Hydration Bladder Additives: We all know that putting "Gatorade" or other electrolyte additives into your hydration bladder will result in bacteria forming in your drink tube/reservoir and could spoil your trip. Camelbak has developed tablets that you add to your water that will replenish your essential electrolytes. They are called Elixirs and they come in flavors and will not develop into bacteria in your hydration bladder. These can also help to make filtered water taste a little better.

Battery Life: Try to keep your items that use the AA or AAA batteries warm. Cold weather shortens the life of the batteries. Instead of leaving the day pack out in the truck, tuck it in the tent or camper where you have heat. Also consider buying the lithium batteries especially for the items that might save your life--GPS, flashlights, etc. They cost more but have proven to last a considerably longer time than the alkaline. Finally, keep a spare set of batteries in a pocket close to your body when you are in the field. Your body heat will help prolong the life of the battery.

Sneaky Footwear: Buy the better quality foot bedsoles (boot insoles) and roll them up in your daypack. When the time comes to put the stalk on an elk slide the bedsoles inside the socks and slip these on to move in for that final few yards needed for the kill. Unless you already have them inside your boots, then just remove them and place inside the socks. Quiet and gives some protection against thorns, sharp rocks, etc.

Camp Chow: In our camp this past year we ate pre-made foods like spaghetti, chili, Sloppy Joes, etc.. And put it in Rubbermaid containers. Worked terrific, however, this year we will be doing the same but using vacuum sealed bags instead.

Hunter #2: We have been using the Stouffers "Skillet Meals" found in the frozen food section at the market. Open the bag, pour it in the skillet. Cover for five to seven minutes. Stir a couple of times. Cover for about five more minutes. Dish out on to plates. About fifteen minutes total cooking time which is great after a long day covering ground to get where the elk like to play and back out again. The older I get the easier I try to make it.

Hunter # 3: We precook everything too. For base camp we'll have stews, casseroles and the like for supper. For breakfast and spike camp groceries we have a different approach. To keep from spreading cooking smells all over the mountain, we pre-cook burritos and wrap them in aluminum foil. For breakfast at base camp they are fast, easy and heat up while getting ready. In spike camp, they can easily be warmed up over a pack stove without having to start a fire. We use the large tortillas, stuffed full of sausage, eggs, cheese, tators, onions, bell peppers, spices and of course a touch of picante sauce. Other variations are fajitas, Swiss steak, thick chili, any recipe that is not too juicy, or whatever your imagination can come up with. We freeze them at home and at spike camp, leave them in the snow or cool place to keep from spoiling.

Camp Map: I know most of you have plans when hunting in parties. Just a reminder or tip for those of you that are new. There are four of us that hunt together every year. In our base camp we have a laminated map of the entire region we hunt. It is posted on the inside of the tent, on the wall. We pair off daily. We have up to four places on the map we mark that shows where we will be. Two of us use blue markings and the other two use red. We mark the color and number them, number 1 being the first choice and so on. We all agree on a liberal time when we all expect to be back at camp. Once that time has passed and someone has not shown up, it is time to act. Whoever is back at camp will start from number 1 and go to 4: If by chance someone comes back to camp and then goes back out to recover game, we leave a note with the numbered location where we are. Simple and it works. The one sticking out for me was this year. I was hunting on a saddle and passed out. It was very close to dark. Hunting partner was heading back to and did not come across me at the truck. He headed to my spot and found me.

Hunter # 2: We use GPS and cell phones. Had a member drop into a bowl last year and had to jump in the truck and drive down seven miles to pick him up on the other side because the terrain was too steep for him to make it back up. Always know where you are before you jump into something or it may be a very long walk back to where you started.

Recipes

For the most part we have included these recipes just as they were given to us. The idea was to leave as much of the individual's flavorful language in the mix as possible. As you will see, some have more 'flavor' than others and that is exactly how we like it. If you have a favorite camp recipe, email it to us at elkmaster@elkcamp.com. Maybe we will include it in a future volume. Enjoy.

Easy Sloppy Joes

This recipe will be a hit at your next outdoor gathering with kids with big appetites.

Brown 1# elk/venison burger
Add
- 1 can of tomato soup

- 1 small jar of salsa (mild or medium - your choice)
Bring to boil then reduce heat & simmer for 30-45 minutes -
Call in the troops and enjoy!

Old Family Favorite

This is one good and easy meal!
1.5 # ground venison/elk
1 can Cream of Mushroom Soup
1 can Chicken Noodle Soup
1 can Chicken Rice Soup
1 can water
1 cup uncooked rice
1 small onion (chopped)
Season Pepper
Soy Sauce

Brown meat along with chopped onion
Add soups, water, rice
Pepper to taste
Soy Sauce to taste (in lieu of salt)
Mix ingredients in pan and place in casserole dish and bake
uncovered @ 350 for 40 min

Elk Roast

1 elk roast
3 jars banana pepper rings
1 pouch Italian dressing (dry)
1 crock pot for 8 or so hours
= priceless

Goose Pate

First debone and cut goose into strips,
Boil until done,

Grind (helps to have a grinder for this one)

Add Spicy Hot Mayo and Smokee Joe Hungarian Seasoning (season with what you want - experiment).

I usually put in the frig overnight, but it tastes pretty dang good right away.

Get out the crackers of your choice and dig in.

Great to go with your beer while you are watching the football game on TV. It's also easy to take along to the field with you and share with your buddies in the box blind or back at the truck.

Wild Turkey Spur Salad

If you like chicken salad (replace with spur salad), a home grown tomato and a cracker, try this excellent recipe WILD TURKEY SPUR SALAD.

Cook a whole, one-half breast of wild turkey in the crock pot over night covered in chicken broth. After cooking all night, remove the wild turkey breast from the broth, cool and then place in the refrigerator overnight (keep whole). The breast needs to be left in the frig over night in order to get firm. If you skip this step, the meat will be mushy. Trust me. I learned the hard way. Firm breast are always the best breast.

After the breast has firmed, then cut the breast in small chunks or cubes.

Mix in a bowl the following ingredients:

- chunked turkey breast
- salt and pepper to personal preference
- take whole sweet pickles (about one cup of chopped pickles) and place in a food chopper to be finely chopped.
- approx 3-4 tablespoons of real mayonnaise (this is not the low fat kind)

optional ingredients
-white grapes cut in half
-slice almonds
After all the ingredients are in the bowl, mix the ingredients
slowly so the meat stays together. After the ingredients are
thoroughly mixed, put it on a Ritz or a homegrown tomato.
It was named Spur Salad at 2007 Elk Camp in Colorado after
stuffing ourselves at lunch while sitting around the camp fire.
True Story!

Mexican Lasagna

Hey campers! Here's a recipe that I came up with last night. I
used ground elk, but you could use deer or antelope, or even
beef if you choose. It's Mexican lasagna that I cooked in my
Dutch oven, but in a regular oven, not with charcoal as one
should with a DO. This recipe was about the perfect size for a
10" DO. My guess is it would work nicely in a 9"x13" casserole
dish if you don't have a 10" DO handy. Anyway, on with the
recipe....

The spices are very approximate, as I made it to my and my
wife's taste. I didn't use the packaged taco seasoning, but
instead came up with my own blend. I could've used some
cumin, but we didn't have any. One thing I should note is that
we buy things that are pretty low in sodium, so naturally they
tend to be fairly bland. The enchilada sauce, corn, beans, and
tortillas were all pretty bland, so I increased the amount of salt
in the dry spices to offset this. Bottom line, you may have to
adjust the amount of spices to suit your taste.

1-2 tsp. salt, depending on taste
1/8 tsp. cayenne pepper
1 tsp. paprika

1 tsp. chili powder

1/8 tsp. freshly ground black pepper

1-2 Tbsp. of olive oil

1/2 med. red onion, finely chopped

3 cloves garlic, minced or finely chopped

1 large jalapeno pepper, seeded and finely chopped

1 lb. ground elk

1 can Mexican corn (the kind with the peppers already mixed in)

2 cans black beans

2 cans Hatch green enchilada sauce

Butter or Crisco to grease the pan

12 to 15 Corn tortillas

1-2 C. of your favorite cheese

Chopped lettuce or cilantro if you desire.

Sour Cream or salsa if you desire.

Preheat the oven to 350 degrees.

1. Heat about 1-2 Tbsp. of olive oil in a 10" cast iron skillet.

2. Brown the onion, jalapeno, and garlic until the onion is slightly cleared.

3. While the onion mixture is browning, brown the ground elk in a 12" cast iron skillet.

4. Once the onion mixture is done, and all the pink is gone from the ground elk, add all of the dry spices, the onion mixture, and the can of Mexican corn to the ground elk. Stir together and let the mixture continue to heat for 5 to 10 minutes.

5. Grease the bottom and sides of the DO with a small amount of Crisco or butter.

6. Put a layer of the corn tortillas in the bottom of the DO.

7. Pour one can of black beans over the tortillas. Spread so they

evenly cover the tortillas.

8. Cover the beans with about half of the ground elk/corn/onion mixture.

9. Pour one can of the green enchilada sauce over the ground elk. Top with about half of the cheese.

10. Add a second layer of the corn tortillas.

11. Add the second can of black beans and spread so they evenly cover the tortillas.

12. Add the remaining ground elk/onion/corn mixture and spread so that it covers the black beans.

13. Top with about half of the second can of green enchilada sauce.

14. Put down another layer of the corn tortillas.

15. Top with the remaining green enchilada sauce and then the remaining cheese.

16. Bake for about 30 minutes or until it's hot and bubbly. Take off the lid of the DO and bake for about 5 more minutes to brown the cheese.

17. After removing from the oven, let it stand for about 5 minutes while everything sets up.

18. Serve hot. If you desire, you can top with some cilantro or lettuce/tomatoes. Sour cream or salsa might also be good. I didn't add either. I used just a dash of hot sauce on top and called it good.

Elk Kabobs

Here's a recipe that we've enjoyed for a while.

2-3 lbs. Elk (or deer) Steaks,

6 pack of beer

1/2 small onion(purple)

4 limes (peeled)

Fajita seasoning

1/2 bell pepper (diced)
1/2 cup fresh cilantro (NO STEMS)
Bacon (cut into 3" pieces)
Toothpicks

1) Sip on 1st of 6-pack
2) Elk steaks (or venison) cut 1/2" thick in approx 2"X3" pieces.
Marinate them in 2nd (a dark) beer, fajita seasoning mix while starting the BBQ pit and fixing the stuffing.
3) Sip on 3rd beer.

4) Stuffing: Peel 4 limes, cut up a 1/2 small onion, 1/2 diced bell pepper, 1/2 cup fresh cilantro, 2 tsp fajita seasoning.
Put this into a chopper/blender and cut to a pulpy, well mixed concoction.
5) Sip on 4th beer.
6) Spoon in 1 (+/-) tsp of this mixture onto the center of the steak then wrap w/ a 3" piece of bacon and skewer w/ a toothpick or shish kabob stick.
7) When charcoals and mesquite (and/or hickory) fire is in medium heat and smoke stage, load up BBQ pit w/ these tasty treats while enjoying beer 5 and 6. Cook until the bacon is crisp or to your liking then ENJOY!

The lime not only has a tenderizing affect but blends in well w/ the onion and cilantro (coriander) and bell pepper to yield a South-West flavor that's hard to beat. This recipe makes enough for five kabobs for four people.

Elk Steak
Rump steaks are great fried or grilled.

I like to use a rub that consists of salt, pepper, garlic powder, onion powder, and a bit of brown sugar (depending on your taste). Paprika and cayenne pepper are also good spices to throw in, depending on what taste you're shooting for.

I let the rub sit on the meat overnight. The next morning, I toss in some olive oil and Worcestershire sauce for a bit of a marinade throughout the day. You can also use some liquid smoke if you like that flavor. The olive oil gives a bit of moisture to the steaks, since wild game is so lean, and I think it helps break down the meat, tenderizing it a bit. This might be just a perception on my part, but it seems to help some.

The key with cooking elk steaks to me is to not overcook them. I would definitely leave them pretty pink instead of fully cooked. Depending on how thick I've cut them, I'll cook a steak about four to seven minutes a side, and that is dependent on how hot your grill/skillet is. If I'm cooking in the skillet, I'll use olive oil, as well. I've read that it's best to not let wild game sit long or "rest" before you dig in, since it doesn't have the fat like beef.

Serve with a green salad, your vegetable of choice, a good slice of bread, and a glass of your favorite pinot noir, and you've got a meal that can't be beat.

Deep Fried Elk Steaks
For those of you that use a turkey fryer...
Heat the peanut oil in the fryer to 325-350 degrees (do not let oil go over 350 as it will start to smoke/break down)

1 pkg of "Shore Lunch" breading

2lbs of tenderized elk steaks
Place breading and steaks in a 1 gallon Ziploc bag. Shake vigorously.
Place breaded steaks in wire basket and slowly lower into oil. REMEMBER: 4 minutes per pound of meat.
After 8 minutes, remove basket of steaks, let drain on paper towel and then serve with a side of baked potato and a salad. (A glass of Chianti goes very well with this too)

Elk Burgers
I use ground elk for burgers from time to time. You have to add a little bit of fat and a binding agent to hold the meat together.
1# ground elk or deer
1 egg
some cracker or bread crumbs to hold the meat together
salt to taste
pepper to taste
garlic salt to taste
whatever other spices you like
a little fat in the form of cheese or olive oil to make them a little moist
sometimes I will add some Worcestershire sauce or liquid smoke to give a little extra flavor

Mix all of this stuff together. Don't overdo the bread or cracker crumbs. I use crackers instead of bread, but it doesn't matter which you use. But don't overdo them because they will overtake the flavor of the other spices you've added. You'll know when you have enough, because the meat will begin to hold together in your hand.

I tend to add a bit more salt than normal to my burgers, but I probably eat more salt than the average Joe.

Cook on medium heat in a skillet or grill to your desired doneness. If in a skillet, I don't add oil. Top with whatever you like, but I use grilled peppers, onions, and mushrooms, and a good slice of provolone cheese between some whole wheat bread or on a good roll. Serve with a cold beer and a good salad, and you're set for the evening.

Chicken Fried Elk Steaks

Here's one of my favorites. You can use this for deer, elk, or any other red meat. I like to use the backstraps for chicken fried steaks, but you can also use rump steaks. You just need to tenderize them a bit.

Sprinkle some salt, black pepper, and garlic powder/salt on the steaks and rub it in good
Let the steaks sit for at least a few hours
Dredge the steaks in an egg/milk mixture
Coat the steaks in a flour mixture containing flour, salt, and black pepper.
Fry in olive oil (or whatever you prefer) in a hot skillet for five to seven minutes per side.

I like to serve this with mashed potatoes, a green salad, and some good bread or biscuits/gravy. What a great southern-style meal.

Elk Chili
Here is one of my family's favorite elk chili recipe.

Please note:
I use a certain ingredient (spice) that is manufactured in Chugwater, Wyoming. This is not an endorsement, just information for a recipe. I am going to include their website in case some would like to try this outstanding recipe.

Ingredients:
2lbs ground elk or deer
1 med onion
1 tsp basil
1/2 tsp oregano
2 cloves garlic, minced
1 large can diced tomatoes
2 (8oz) cans tomato sauce
1 (16oz) can kidney beans
1 c. water
1 packet or 3 tbs. of 'Chugwater Chili" spice

Cook meat until pinkness is gone
Add remaining ingredients and meat into a Crockpot
Simmer for 2-3 hrs

Serves 6-8 (salt and pepper to taste)
http://www.chugwaterchili.com/
(Chugwater Chili is the prize-winning recipe that won the Wyoming State Chili Cook-Off Championship two consecutive years!)

Pheasant Pilaf

I can't claim this one as my own. My son Dan thought this one up... mmm...good.

Ingredients:
3- 4 pheasant or Quail would be good too
1 box Rice a Roni rice pilaf
1 can Ro-Tel mild
vegetable oil
Marjoram spice flakes
Salt and pepper

Start by cooking the rice as per instructions on box. When rice is almost done add half can Ro-Tel and let simmer, prepare pheasant or quail breasted seems to work well, salt and pepper a bit along with Marjoram flakes and coat birds well. A bit of vegetable oil to pan and cook birds until browned about 5-6 min per side. As birds are half done add other half of Ro-Tel into frying pan, it really adds color and flavor. Serve with rice and your favorite veggie. Serves three to four people. If you don't like it so spicy add less Ro-Tel. Be prepared to serve seconds. Gives ya a good reason to go hunting again for more birds.

Ol' Arky's ELK CHILI

Ya can make this in whatever "alarm" ya want by addin' a bit more hot stuff or a bit less but here's mine... I consider it "1 alarm"...

In a medium size pot mix a small can a tomato paste with a large can a tomato sauce startin' to cook over med heat. Fill the tomato paste can half full a hot water mixin' till ya get most all the goody that was left in it, then pour that in the tomato sauce can mixin' till ya get all most all the goody outa it... Pour that into the chili pot too. Fill the tomato sauce can about half full again with hot water mixin' and gettin' the rest a the goody out it... If by chance ya still got a bit a tomato paste left in the other can and if ya wanta ya can pour the last hot water back and forth between cans till totally clean. Pour this in the pot also. Mix a bit... Add a teaspoon or so a ground Cumin, a bit less than a teaspoon a ground Red (Cayenne) Pepper... Mix a bit... Chop a half a good size onion (Ya choice here but I like purple or yellow) and add to the mixture.... Add a big can a Bush's Pinto beans, a regular can a Original Ranch Style beans, a can a MILD Ro-Tel and a can or two a diced tomatoes . By now ya know how to get all the goody outa the cans. Stir the mix for a bit. In another skillet gently cook somewhere around 2 or 3 pounds a ground elk seasoned with a bit a salt, a bit a pepper and a bit a Tony Chachere's Creole Seasonin'... I usually use some that non stick cookin' spray in my elk meat skillet. When the elk is near bout done, dump it in the chili pot. Now pour a half a package a William's Chili seasonin' in on top a mix and stir up real good.... turn up heat and bring it to a boil all the time stirrin' a bit here and there. Then reduce heat to where the chili just bubbles ever once in a while. Cover and cook for ever how long ya need to satisfy yaself it's done (hint: it's done pretty soon after ya brought it to a boil but folks like to cook chili for a while just to smell it cookin')... If it seems a bit "loose" for ya just add some Hunt's tomato ketchup till ya get it thick enough to suit ya taste.

That oughta make enough Ol' Arky's Elk Chili to feed a family a four or eight for a day or two.... Mosta the time a bit longer....

HUNT CONNECTIONS

1 Since 1996

BIG GAME HUNTING CONSULTANTS

North America   Canada   Africa

www.HuntConnections.com

888-360-HUNT (4868)
jay@huntconnections.com

ELK HUNTING IS OUR SPECIALTY